Randall Jorde Covill

Implementing Extranets

The Internet as a
Virtual Private
Network

Digital Press

Implementing Extranets

Implementing Extranets
The Internet as a Virtual Private Network

Randall Jorde Covill

dp

Digital Press

Boston • Oxford • Johannesburg • Melbourne • New Delhi • Singapore

Library of Congress Cataloging-in-Publication Data

Covill, Randall J.
    Implementing extranets : the Internet as a virtual private network
/ by Randall Jorde Covill.
      p.   cm.
    Includes bibliographical references and index.
    ISBN 1-55558-197-8 (alk. paper)
     1. Extranets (Computer networks)   2. Virtual proprietary networks.
I. Title.
HD30.382.C68   1998
650'.0285'46—dc21   98-23427
                                          CIP

British Library Cataloguing-in-Publication Data

A catalogue record for this book is available from the British Library.

The publisher offers special discounts on bulk orders of this book.
For information, please contact:
Manager of Special Sales
Butterworth–Heinemann
225 Wildwood Avenue
Woburn, MA 01801-2041
Tel: 781-904-2500
Fax: 781-904-2620

For information on all Butterworth–Heinemann publications available, contact our World Wide Web home page at: http://www.bh.com

Order number: EY-V420E-DP

10 9 8 7 6 5 4 3 2 1

Printed in the United States of America

This book is dedicated to my wife Nancy, my friends Churchill and Baxter, and my editors Liz McCarthy and Pam Chester.

Contents

Preface   ix

1 Introduction   1

2 A Return on Investment Analysis   7

3 The Challenges of Using Extranets   35

4 Access Solutions for Extranets   55

5 Highly Available and Reliable Extranets   81

6 Extranet Security   95

7 Extranet Performance   123

8 Managing Extranets   139

9 Administering Extranets   151

10 Future Challenges and Directions of Extranets   161

11 Deciding Whether or Not to Implement an Extranet   177

Bibliography   195

Index   199

Preface

I wanted to write this book because I have a passionate interest in the way that people design, implement, and use new technologies to improve their lives. Internets, intranets, and extranets all fascinate me because they are tools for creating on-line, electronic, or virtual communities.

The news sometimes reports the breakdown of this or that "real" as opposed to "virtual" community. If community is defined as a set or collection of people who share common interests, fantasies, and transactions and who communicate or relate regularly then I am happy to report that the on-line type of communities known as extranets, intranets, and Internet are growing, thriving, and experiencing ever larger numbers of members.

Moreover, virtual or on-line communities can be used to strengthen and unite off-line or real life communities. Even the British royal family has an Internet site that received 35 million visits in the two weeks after Princess Diana's death. According to news reports, the royal Internet site received about 80 million visits in its first eight months of operation.

Anyone who is interested in how extranets are designed and implemented should read this book. Anyone who wants to know whether or not extranets are ready for prime time or to provide infrastructure and support for mission-critical business applications should read this book and then draw their own conclusions. In addition, anyone who wants to understand the opportunities, challenges, and solutions that are part of designing and implementing extranets should read this book.

But most of all, anyone who wants to take a look at the new and exciting technology that makes the on-line business communities, known as extranets, possible will enjoy this book!

I especially want to thank my friends and colleagues from Digital Equipment Corporation and Digital Press for the opportunity to study, learn, and write about many new and exciting technologies and business processes over the years! I would also like to thank Daniel Dern, a columnist and author of books on the Internet and mobile computing, for carefully reviewing an earlier version of this manuscript and suggesting improvements to it. Any remaining deficiencies are solely my own.

1

Introduction

Chapter Objectives

The goals of this chapter are to:

▶ explain why and for whom I wrote this book,

▶ define the terms "Internet as a virtual private network" and "extranet," and

▶ to describe the lessons learned from an early use of the extranet.

In later chapters of this book, we'll explore the extranet and the performance, security, capacity, management, and administration issues that surround it in more detail.

Why I Wrote This Book and Who I Wrote It For

A central theme of this and my other book, *Migrating to the Intranet and Microsoft Exchange*, is that the major business challenges of today involve forecasting, decision making, and focus. Successfully meeting these challenges requires information access, information sharing, and collaboration. In other words, information technology can deliver tangible benefits to end users, managers, and businesses.

In this book, my focus is on how individuals as well as businesses can benefit from extranets. Thus, I have included descriptions of how individuals as well as businesses are using extranets to achieve success. In general, my business focus is on large enterprises. However, I will frequently discuss small and medium enterprises as well in order to better illustrate my points. I don't know of any rigorous definition of small, medium, and large enterprises so I will make up my own.

In my view, a large enterprise is one with many thousands of employees and end users of technology spread across many geographic locations. To me, a medium enterprise is one with a few thousand employees spread

1

across several geographic locations, and a small enterprise is one with less than a thousand employees in one or two locations. Often, but not always, the larger the enterprise the more complex the technology environment of the enterprise.

The Great Controversy

I especially wrote this book because of my strong interest in exploring and understanding what I call the great Internet as a virtual private network controversy. In other words, many businesses are saying to themselves "Why should we spend a lot of money to extend the infrastructure of our proprietary networks to communicate with remote branch offices and factories, suppliers, and business partners? Why don't we use the Internet to do that job instead?" On the other hand, many authors and end users are saying that the Internet so lacks access, security, performance, capacity, scalability, ease of use, and ability to enable business transactions that it will never replace proprietary networks.

The Internet as a Virtual Private Network or Extranet

Unfortunately acronyms and conflicting definitions abound in books on computers and technology; thus, it's important to understand how each author defines his or her terms. To me, using the Internet as a virtual private network or extranet really refers to taking information that originally was designed to travel across a proprietary network and therefore has a proprietary wrapper and compressing it, encrypting it, and placing it in a TCP/IP wrapper so that it can travel or "tunnel" across the Internet. It travels to a destination where it will be unwrapped, decompressed, de-encrypted, and used in some private or business setting. Figure 1.1 is a representation of such doubly wrapped information solutions.

The technology that does all of this is what enables corporations to open their Intranet web sites to suppliers, contractors, consultants, customers, and other stakeholders. The network that results from the opening of proprietary or private web sites to a bounded set of outsiders in order to share information and collaborate with them is an "extranet." Figure 1.2 is a pictorial representation of an extranet.

To me, the terms "extranets" and "Internets as virtual private networks" refer to very similar ideas so I will use the terms interchangeably. Although "extranet" was originally a term found in business-oriented discussions and the "Internet as a virtual private network" was found in technology-oriented discussions, the two terms are coming to mean the same thing—namely, using

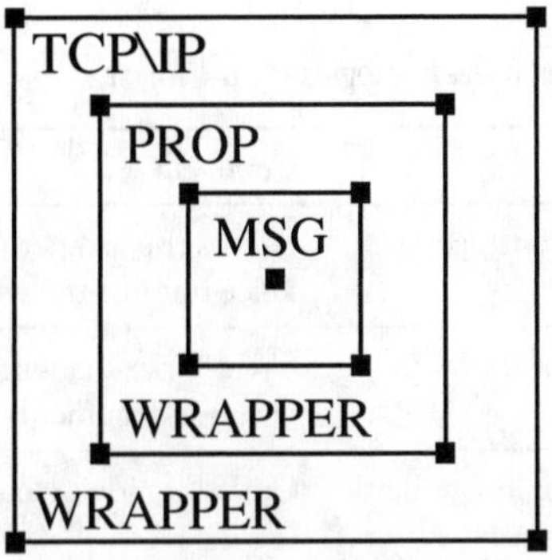

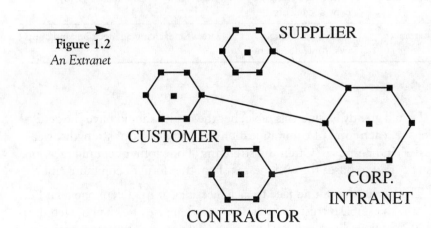

Figure 1.1
*An Extranet
Wrapper*

TCP\IP

PROP

MSG

WRAPPER

WRAPPER

Figure 1.2
An Extranet

SUPPLIER

CUSTOMER

CONTRACTOR

CORP.
INTRANET

Internet technology to communicate, collaborate, and share information with some bounded set of business partners both inside and outside the enterprise. The set of business partners needs to be bounded or a "public network" and not an "extranet" results. If the set of people with access to web sites are all employees then an intranet results. Thus public networks are open to everyone without restriction. Extranets are open only to a bounded set of suppliers and business partners, and intranets are open only to employees.

Using Complementary Communication and Information Technologies

I do not believe that the extranet is so much a substitute for other forms of communication as it is a complement to other forms of communication. For example, Table 1.1 shows the primary purposes for which different communication and collaboration technologies were used during the lifetime of a project.

Table 1.1   *Uses of Multiple Communication Technologies for a Project*

Technology	Uses	Comment
1. Telephone	Build relationships Establish trust	Allows the listener to hear the tone of voice not just the words
2. Fax	Exchange of short documents	Great for exchanging and signing legal and business documents
3. Overnight Services	Exchange of longer hard copy documents	Great for moving hard copy quickly
4. U.S. Mail	Exchange of longer hard copy documents	Great for moving hard copy slowly
5. Extranet	Exchange of longer electronic documents	Great for exchanging mock ups and drafts

I could greatly extend this table, but the reader should have the general idea, i.e. each form of communication has its own set of strengths, weaknesses, and best uses. Often the strengths of one form of communications can be used to offset the weaknesses of another form of communication.

This author has found face to face meetings or the telephone a far better way to establish trust and relationships than use of e-mail or web sites. The U.S. mails have proven to be an effective way to move hard copy when time is not of the essence, and overnight services (e.g., FedEx) have proven to be an effective way to move hard copy when time is of the essence. The extranet has shown itself to be a very effective way to move e-mail and electronic documents between insiders and outsiders to the networked or virtual enterprise. All of these things work well and deliver the best results when used effectively together.

A Note on the Statistics in This Book and Extranet Time

In the world of the Internet and extranets, many things double in size or speed every 18 months; nevertheless, the statistics in this book remain useful, if conservative, indicators of the Internet's and extranets' trends.

Chapter Summary and Lessons Learned

This chapter explained why I wrote this book; who I wrote it for; the common themes of this book; how I define small, medium, and large enterprise, extranet, and the Internet as a virtual private network. I'll finish this chapter with some practical advice for you in the form of a list of lessons learned from my first attempt to use the extranet on a real live business project. In the next chapter, we'll explore the great Internet as a Virtual Private Network Controversy in more detail and set the stage for a discussion in subsequent chapters about how you can use the Internet as a virtual private network today.

Table 1.2 summarizes what I learned upon using an extranet to communicate with writers and suppliers to produce sales literature at one-third the cost and one-third the time of previous projects without an extranet.

Table 1.2 *Lessons Learned from a First Use of an Extranet*

Business and Project Management Lessons

1. An extranet can greatly increase the speed and effectiveness of sharing information in the form of project goals, project plans, project status reports, project strategy, project assessments, solutions to problems, and drafts of content with both authorized corporate insiders and authorized corporate outsiders like consultants, contractors, suppliers, etc.

2. Sensible use of an extranet by those people familiar with technology really can shorten cycle time and increase the odds of meeting aggressive project budgets and schedules.

3. Multiple communication and information technologies can be used to complement each other and to therefore reduce the risk of relying on any single technology exclusively.

4. Peer reviews and walk throughs of drafts can be a very effective quality control mechanism.

5. Weekly or even more frequent milestones can be an effective way to keep an aggressive project on track.

6. Project team wide visibility of progress against plan can also be a very effective way of keeping an aggressive project on track.

7. Configuration management or version control is an important part of project success which the extranet and web sites can help a great deal with.

8. Triage, triage, and triage again is the key to success on an extremely aggressive project. Triage is more effective than new technology, silver bullets, or even friends and sponsors in high places!

Technology Lessons

1. The telephone is far better than the extranet when it's necessary to listen to people and to gauge their emotional state.

2. There remain significant concerns with extranet accessibility, security, performance, capacity, ease of use, scalability, and as an enabler of business transactions and applications.

Table 1.2 *Lessons Learned from a First Use of an Extranet (Continued)*

Technology Lessons (Continued)

3. An extremely aggressive production project is not a good time to introduce new technology to the team. However, the learning curve risk can be decreased if the team is familiar with similar technologies.

4. Don't even bother to try to e-mail or move large documents off web sites and across the extranet without compressing them first! Uncompressed files never made it across the network without truncation or other damage.

People Lessons

1. The extranet is pretty much useless when it comes to establishing trust for the first time between strangers.

2. If I ever had to choose between good people and good technology to get the job done, I'd choose the people each and every time.

3. On a very aggressive, high-pressure project it's more important than ever to frequently take the emotional temperature of the team and to work hard to build trust and the extraordinary commitment required to make the project a success.

4. Isolate the team from bureaucratic and administrative distractions.

5. Avoid project reviews by unprepared, but loud, reviewers. It will not be productive!

Personal Lessons

1. The extranet and other new technologies erode the boundary between personal life and work life requiring people to make much more frequent, personal, and serious decisions about balancing life and work.

2. Technology users need to devote more time and energy to balancing work and personal life than ever before.

3. Don't give up running. The more intense the project the more you will need the exercise!

4. Sun-Tzu knew what he was talking about when he wrote *The Art of Warfare*. The book is full of strategy that can be applied to any project or human endeavor in which strategy matters!

2

A Return on Investment Analysis

Chapter Objectives

In Chapter 1, I gave you some definitions and lessons learned from using extranets. I hope that the previous chapter convinced you that there are some very significant business benefits to be gained by using the Internet as a virtual private network or extranet. (The terms *Internet as a virtual private network*, *virtual private network (VPN)*, and *extranet* are used as synonyms throughout this book.)

In Chapter 2, we're going to switch gears a bit, become more technical, and examine the technology issues that are driving the costs, benefits, and return on investment analysis of using the Internet as a virtual private network. In examining these issues, you will develop a feel for the exciting possibilities, challenges, and changes going on around the Internet as a virtual private network. The objectives of this chapter are to:

▶ Discuss the cost drivers associated with using an extranet.

▶ Discuss some of the benefits that can be derived from using an extranet.

▶ Discuss the total cost of using an extranet and the effects of shifting cost from one of the elements of total cost to other elements.

▶ Give you some sample templates and tools that you can use to perform your own return on investment analysis of using the Internet as an extranet.

▶ Help you develop your own return on investment analysis and forecast of benefits and costs of using the Internet as an extranet.

Putting forecasts of benefits and costs and return on investment analysis in perspective should make this chapter more fun and interesting to read. In addition, perspective needs to be discussed and understood if the tools discussed in this chapter are to be used properly and effectively. Also, seeing things in perspective or in context is an important part of knowing where you are and where you want to go.

Putting Things in Perspective

At more than one industry conference and business meeting I've heard someone state that, "These numbers are all made up!" That's exactly right and as it should be!

To do an effective job of forecasting benefits and costs for a return on investment analysis you need to "make up" or select the most accurate numbers that best fit your own unique technical and business environment. This is the only way that that your forecast and analysis has any chance at all of being relevant to what you are attempting to do.

I've also heard it said many in times in high tech markets that short-term forecasts are usually extremely overly optimistic and long-term forecasts are usually extremely overly pessimistic. In other words, it is usually harder to successfully complete any short-term project than anyone imagined and the results of technology improvements over the long term often greatly exceeds everyone's expectations!

The Internet itself is a perfect example of this principle in action. The first Internet was built more than 25 years ago, but only in the last five years or so has the Internet truly captured public and media attention.

You should also be less concerned with getting your numbers right than with understanding and clearly stating the arguments and assumptions behind your forecast of benefits and costs and return on investment analysis. Understanding the arguments, assumptions, and directions of forecasts and analysis are often more valuable and important than the actual numbers used in the forecast and analysis. Using the templates and tools described in this chapter will not only help you make a rational decision about whether or not to use an extranet but will also help you understand and appreciate many of the technology and business elements that make up a virtual private network.

You can use this understanding to derive even more benefits from an extranet as well as to lower costs. Many of the cost drivers and benefits and their interactions described in this chapter will be described in much greater detail in future chapters. In fact, our discussion of cost drivers, cost elements, and benefits will be a good introduction to many of the scalability, performance, security, and manageability issues that have made extranets controversial!

Let's begin at the beginning by discussing constraints and costs for getting connected to the Internet in the first place.

Internet Access as a Cost Driver of Using the Internet as a Virtual Private Network

To successfully access the Internet several things are required. First of all, everyone accessing and using the Internet as a virtual private network must have access to a computer of their own or of someone else's through school, work, libraries, cyber cafes, or whatever. You do not necessarily need access to a fully loaded PC with hard drive and lots of local cache memory. A dumb terminal will do fine if you have the right software for it. A net PC running a browser or Internet client software will also work fine. (See the section later in this chapter on client server configurations and cost shifting for a definition and discussion of net PCs.)

The computer that you use to access the Internet will have a significant impact on both the cost of and benefits achievable from your use of an extranet. For example, dumb terminal or shell access to the Internet once was the most inexpensive access, but is now available from a diminishing number of Internet Service Providers (ISPs). Fees could run as low as $15–$30 per month per account for unlimited usage. Shell access means that the computer or dumb terminal accessing the Internet is in reality sending commands to another computer which is actually attached to the Internet and running programs related to the Internet. What this means is that shell access to the Internet although inexpensive is sometimes restricted to exchanging text only with other computers on the Internet. This may or may not matter to you depending on what you want to use the Internet for. For example, traveling sales reps may or may not be happy to use the Internet for the exchange of text based e-mail only in which case shell and dumb terminal access is good enough.

On the other hand, your user community may want far more from the Internet and your network than the exchange of text only. Sales reps, marketing managers, field service engineers, suppliers, customers, and others who travel frequently or roam about or move from a territory covered by one Internet Service Provider to a territory covered by another Internet Service Provider may want access to graphics, pictures, and sound as well as text. If this is the case then your users will need SLIP (serial line interface protocol) or PPP (peer to peer protocol) access which are now the dominant offerings from Internet Service Providers. These access protocols enable the user's machine to run programs that can directly access the Internet and receive audio, video, and text files from the Internet.

You will need either a local, regional, or national Internet Service Provider to connect your users to the Internet. Both local and national ISPs often offer 800 number access which can be a money saver for users who travel often and frequently dial into the ISP via a long distance call. Moreover, there are Point of Presence or POP sharing consortia like Ipass and GRIC which give companies and individuals affordable use of POPs that belong to other ISPs.

However, the good news is that heavy competition among Internet ISPs is forcing down the cost of accessing the Internet. Many ISPs and online service providers have adopted flat rates for monthly access up to some time limit. For example, an ISP might charge 20 dollars for up to 100 hours of Internet connect time per month. America Online was the first to do this and attracted so much business that it has had to dramatically upgrade its network. The online service providers often provide content and information in addition to Internet access in return for their fees. Although frequently more expensive than local ISPs, the online service providers offer more to the user than just Internet access. Online service providers like America Online, Prodigy, CompuServe, etc., often offer detailed business, legal, and technical information online that may not be available from any other source. However the online service providers clearly feel challenged by the richness of information that the Internet and World Wide Web have to offer. The right kind of ISP or ISPs for you very much depends upon what you want to use the Internet for.

Internet Service Providers are increasingly offering blocking, filtering, and reporting services to those who pay for their services. This means that as an employer wanting to ensure that employees use the Internet only for business purposes you can ask the Internet Service Provider to block user access to specific Internet addresses, or to filter by delivering certain types of information to users only when certain parameters are satisfied (like use of a company credit card), or to provide you regular reports and audit trails on the type of information accessed by users. Blocking and filtering are clearly forms of censorship and reporting is thought by some to be an invasion of privacy. Thus blocking, filtering, and reporting are highly controversial subjects. Some employers have stayed away from blocking, filtering, and reporting but ask employees to sign a contract in which they promise not to abuse Internet access. If someone violates their contract, they lose their Internet Service Provider account and can no longer access the Internet. Other employers trust their employees to do the right thing.

This "do the right thing" approach is often followed in highly creative and technical environments. Blocking, filtering, and reporting are clearly as much issues of ethics and politics as of Internet Service Provider expense.

Client Server Configurations as a Cost Driver of Using an Extranet

As the following two tables show, the use of different client server configurations in using an extranet shifts cost to different elements of the network. Total cost may or may not change, but changing configurations can shift both initial and ongoing costs.

As you can see from these tables it is much easier to shift cost elements around than it is to reduce total costs. Although the cost of a net PC is often much less than the cost of a fully loaded PC ($500 vs. $3,000 or so), much of the cost advantage of the net PC disappears when the total cost of the entire networked solution (network, servers, and net PCs) is

Table 2.1 *A Summary of Cost Locations for Different Computing Configurations*

PC Only	All of the hardware, software, and support costs are on the PC
Fat Client/Thin Server	Most costs are on the desktop client with less cost on the server and the network
Thin Client/Fat Server	Most costs are on the server with less cost on the desktop client and the network
Net PC	Most costs are on the network with less cost on the net PC and servers. A net PC can be thought of as a programmable terminal as opposed to a dumb terminal.

Table 2.2 *Cost Elements and Cost Shifting Opportunities*

1. Client and server startup costs. For example, license fees per user, per client, and per server; hardware for clients and servers; migration and training costs, etc.

2. Network backbone and inter-enterprise hardware and software costs. For example, firewalls, application gateways, and directory services, etc.

3. Internal installation and upgrade costs. For example, the cost of upgrading desktop PCs or servers, etc.

4. Ongoing costs. For example, client and server software, hardware, and maintenance costs; server, and network administrative costs.

5. System security and integrity maintenance, help desk, and network usage costs.

considered. This is especially true when the ongoing costs of management and administration of all elements of the networked solution are considered.

You should be aware that the start-up cost of using an extranet is likely to decrease rapidly in the future as the cost of tunneling and security software products decline as well as the cost of PCs decline. However, low-cost net PCs are unlikely to satisfy power users or those who wish to work off line much of the time generating and storing data as they work alone.

One of the major mistakes to avoid in determining the true or total cost of any network or client server solution is to confuse initial or start-up costs that you pay only once with maintenance, support, administrative, or management costs, which you must pay for on an ongoing basis. Choosing to minimize up front one-time costs while increasing ongoing costs is very likely to be an expensive mistake. Special care should be taken in shifting costs from the one time start-up category to the ongoing maintenance, support, system administration, or system management categories.

In some circles, there is a very confusing and muddled debate going on around the relative cost of Internet-based vs. client server-based solutions. The confusion comes from the fact that Internet-based solutions are a kind of client server-based solution. The Internet paradigm of browsers interacting with web servers that interact with application or data base servers is a client server paradigm of computing. If there is any difference between the client server and Internet paradigms of computing, it has to do with the use of thin clients, browsers, or net PCs vs. fully loaded PCs.

The use of thin clients or net PCs may be one way to control costs. Net PCs are stripped down PCs that get their applications and software from a network instead of their own hard drive. Thus, they cost only $300–$500 as compared to a $2,500–$4,000 fully loaded PC that does similar functions. However much of the cost difference between net PCs and fully loaded PCs evaporates if the cost of building and maintaining a network is included in the cost of the net PCs. The real advantage of using light clients and net PCs is that it becomes much easier to control and implement software maintenance and upgrades over the network rather than by physically visiting each PC on a desktop. Gartner Group has estimated the annual cost of managing, administering, and upgrading a fully loaded PC at approximately $8,000 per user. This is an amount that many enterprises and individuals hope to lower by going to a centralized and remote management of net PCs. Moreover, net PCs are likely to increase the ease of use and productivity of PCs in general since users will not have to fool around with the operating system to make things work.

Increased ease of use is something that at least some PC users fervently desire. I have talked to many PC users who are tired of having to deal with the complexities of PC operating systems and of struggling with their PCs to make things work. These are users who feel that their employers are paying them to do something other than to struggle with their PC operating system. These users would welcome the remote software upgrades and management offered by net PCs.

PC productivity and usability could use some improvement. For example, at the Spring 1997 Client Server Data Base World exposition in Boston it was reported that one study had revealed that PCs in homes spent 52% of the time doing nothing when turned on, 18% of the time being maintained or debugged, 18% of the time word processing, and 10% of the time running games. In effect, the PCs were idle or being fixed 70% of the time that they were turned on!

The Internet is likely to be a major player in the net PC game because web servers are likely to be the source of most of the software, applications, and data run on the net PCs.

In the evolution of clients and servers from heavy clients to stored procedures on servers to lighter and lighter clients with more and more functionality and data stored on servers, the Internet is likely to be a key catalyst of change.

Moreover, the relatively low cost of TCP/IP networking at least as compared to networking with proprietary protocols ($7,000 per month for an ISP connection as opposed to $20,000 per month for a T1 line according to one example cited at Client Server Data Base World in Boston) is likely to support the cost savings offered by net PCs. However, the movement to net PCs is expected to take time. The figures mentioned at Client Server Data Base World were only a 2%–4% market penetration of net PCs by the year 2000 primarily as replacements for IBM 3270 dumb terminals.

Enterprise Cost Drivers of Using the Internet as an Extranet

Many of the significant cost drivers of an extranet are not very different from the cost drivers for enterprise class solutions in general. An extranet spans business units and different geographic locations. In addition, it must be scalable in that it can grow to handle more traffic as the volume of traffic grows. It must be highly reliable because many employees, customers, suppliers, and transactions will depend upon it; and it must be extensible in that new functionality can be easily added to it.

Extensibility is an especially important requirement given the increasing speed with which business rules change causing business applications to change. Adaptive systems readily incorporate changes in business rules and are by definition easily extensible systems.

Certainly an extranet needs to be an adaptive or easily extensible system.

All of these requirements cost money to design and implement. However, these costs can be kept down by implementing component or modular design techniques and by implementing industry standard interfaces between components. The use of industry standard interfaces between components means that commodity low cost components can often be used in the system. Reusable code modules lower the cost of developing new functionality. The use of standard interfaces makes the system more easily extensible in that new functionality can be more easily added. Modular design makes it easier to add newer and more powerful modules in order to scale up the system, and the encapsulation of specific functionality into modules makes the system more reliable. See Ed Yourdon's book *Object Oriented Systems Design: An Integrated Approach* for a more detailed discussion of this topic.

Although code reuse is a great idea in terms of increasing programmer productivity and code quality, actual implementation of code reuse has been slow to catch on because most programmers are still paid and rewarded to write new code modules not to reuse older code modules. However, the widespread availability of off-the-shelf dynamic linking and loading code libraries and of frameworks or containers for the dynamic linking and loading code libraries is leading to a growing market for reusable code. The growth of this market is likely to result in lower costs for developing web-enabled enterprise application software.

Although proprietary wide area networks are often viewed by their supporters as being more secure, reliable, and of higher performance than an extranet, there is little disagreement that the proprietary wide area networks are more expensive to develop and operate than is a TCP/IP network. This author has heard estimates as high as 10 cents per kilobyte to move information across wide area proprietary networks as networking seminars and conferences! The costs of moving information across the Internet is far less than this.

Growth and Scalability as Cost Drivers of Using the Internet as a Virtual Private Network

It is also interesting to observe that enormous growth applies to most things around the Internet. For example, PacBell revealed at the Fall 1997 Networld/Interop meeting that Internet traffic is growing 15% per year in California. This means that the total amount of Internet traffic on PacBell's California network will double in about five years. In addition, data traffic will exceed voice traffic on their network. PacBell is hoping to use the Internet as a virtual private network to separate the voice from the data traffic to alleviate network congestion.

Internet traffic is not growing equally fast everywhere however. For example, PacBell indicated that 40% of all Internet traffic originates or terminates in California, 6% originates or terminates in Texas, and 5% originates or terminates in Massachusetts. What all of this clearly implies is that any one implementing an extranet needs to plan for substantial growth in traffic and use of the network. Spending more to acquire scalable solutions that can handle additional traffic as use of the network grows is fully justifiable. However, the single greatest cost driver of using the Internet as an extranet is very likely to be the cost of real and perceived security.

Security Cost Drivers of Using the Internet as an Extranet

It is important to understand that the perceived state of Internet security is just as important as the real state of security when it comes to doing business over the Internet.

Many people believe that sending their credit card number over the Internet places them at large financial risk even though if their card number is stolen and used by a thief the card's legitimate owner is only liable for the first $50 of fraudulent charges. Much of the perceived risk is clearly a matter of branding and image. After all, most of the large stock and bond brokers have web sites that customers can visit to conduct transactions and to check the status of their accounts. Customers do not perceive these sites to be insecure at least partly because customers believe that the companies that maintain those sites have gone to great lengths to make them secure.

What all of this means, is that to successfully use the Internet as a virtual private network or extranet connecting employees, customers, and suppliers you will have to spend money on perceived as well as real security. You will have to ensure that users of your network perceive the network to be secure in addition to actually making it secure.

ATM machines and ATM networks have been very successful in terms of perceived as well as real security. The ATM model of access to your money from anywhere but controlled and managed from a central location by a bank or financial institution has generated a belief in the mind of the public that ATM transactions are safe and secure.

You need to strive for a similar perception on the part of network users in order to use the Internet as a virtual private network or extranet. In other words, you need to market the safety and security of your network to network users! The Internet Travel network successfully did this when it became part of American Express and put American Express in its name. Because of the new name, users believed that transactions were secure and business exploded after the name change.

As was stated in one of the seminars at the Spring 1997 Networld/ Interop, 80% of the security threat to enterprise networks comes from within the organization itself and only about 20% of the security threat to enterprise networks comes from outside the organization. In terms of cost, this implies that much of the security-related costs of using the Internet as a virtual private network would have to be born by an enterprise with multiple networks anyway in order to protect its networks and systems from attacks from within.

For example, the standard elements of any computer and network security program or policy are authentication, access control, data integrity, and data confidentiality. Regardless of whether or not the enterprise chooses to implement local and wide area communications with or without the Internet as a virtual private network, it will have to spend money in order to implement these elements of network and computer security or run the legal, social, and economic risks of operating unsecured systems and networks.

Using the Internet as an extranet does add some cost to securing systems and networks, but not all that much. For example, the enterprise will probably purchase routers or firewalls to filter packets between networks via addresses, port numbers, and content or via states and circuits regardless of whether or not there is an extranet in place in the organization. Proxy servers, dual homed hosts, and subnets are likely to be implemented to establish security between business units, functions, and organizational units of the enterprise regardless of the Internet. Most enterprises want to ensure that e-mail between the chief executive officer and chief financial officer of the enterprise about possible future mergers and acquisitions is secret and secure from reading by most employees.

However, use of extranets to link different business units across the enterprise or to support an extranet usually means that security policies like blocking messages from all suspect addresses at the firewall will not work. Instead, selective penetration of the firewall by messages from different business units and suppliers is often required. Likewise, blocking of messages based upon default addresses will not work if employees are trying to legitimately cross the firewall while roaming or traveling because addresses are dynamically allocated to roaming employees so no one can know what address might be legitimate until roaming employees actually try to link up and tunnel through the firewall.

Thus, you should expect to pay for some of the more sophisticated security tools and processes like data encryption during transmission and storage while implementing an extranet. If security technologies are properly designed and implemented, they do indeed result in highly secure networks.

In addition, you should expect firewall scalability requirements to be a significant driver of expense. In the past, typical scalability solutions have usually involved putting in another box and hiring someone to run it. This was because packet filtering at the firewall was usually a strictly sequential process with no provision for parallel processing, multithreading, or concurrent processes and connections. A lot of research is being done to implement parallel processing, multithreading, and clustering of hardware in the sense of resource sharing for firewalls. Thus, you can expect scalability solutions to get better, faster, and to come down in price as time passes.

The need for ever more powerful solutions to security issues and problems is often driven by the business and legal need to keep extensive logs and audit trails. Security logs can grow rapidly. They not only have to be archived regularly but also examined and retrieved regularly so that if there is in fact a security problem action can and will be taken immediately. Likewise, there is a great need for intrusion detection tools so that immediate action can be taken in the event of a breach of network or system security. As was discussed in the previous section, scalability is a cost driver of using the Internet as an extranet. Given the explosive growth of traffic and other things associated with the Internet, it makes sense to use the most powerful hardware and software available when implementing your firewalls and network security solutions for using the Internet as an extranet.

Use of the Internet as an extranet is based upon Transmission Control Protocol/Internet Protocol (TCP/IP) networking. Thus, the cost of using and securing the Internet as an extranet is closely related to the cost of using and securing TCP/IP networks. If you are already familiar with and are securing the elements of the TCP/IP protocol stack (e.g., physical layer, data link layer, network or IP layer, transport layer, and application layer) then the cost of using and securing the Internet as an extranet may not be that much more.

The following tables describe the TCP/IP layers and how firewalls and routers relate to TCP/IP layers. Information on the Open Systems Interconnection protocol (OSI) is included as well because in many ways TCP/IP is a kind of subset of the OSI protocol.

As you can see from the tables different layers of the protocols provide different network functions and each of these functions provides opportunities for and required protection from breaches of security. The last table relates certain kinds of security attacks to specific security devices. These protocols allow different computers and machines to communicate by establishing and implementing the rules of communication. Future chapters will deal with the Internet as an extranet security issues in far greater detail than these tables describe.

Table 2.3 *Transmission Control Protocol Internet Protocol (TCP/IP) Layers, Open Systems Interconnection (OSI) Layers, and Security Devices*

Security Device	TCP/IP Layer	OSI Layer
Firewall		Application Layer
Firewall		Presentation Layer
Firewall	Application Layer	Session Layer
Firewall and Router	Transport Layer	Transport Layer
	(Transmission Control Protocol)	
	(User Datagram Protocol)	
Firewall and Router	Network Layer	Network Layer
	(Internet Protocol)	
	Data Link Layer	Data Link Layer
	Physical Layer	Physical Layer

Table 2.4 *Summary of Functionality Provided by Protocol Layers*

Layer	Functionality
Application Layer	Consumes services from lower layers via application programming interfaces
Presentation Layer	Presents different data types
Session Layer	Provides end-to-end communication via full duplex, half duplex, and one-way services
Transport Layer	Provides multiplexing, connectionless and connection-oriented services
Network Layer	Extends data link layer services to incompatible networks via routing and protocol conversion
Data Link Layer	Groups bits into frames for error detection and flow control
Physical Layer	Manages the physics of binary bit streams

Table 2.5 *Types of Security Attacks*

Firewall Attacks	Application gateway attacks, server filters, and application programming interface attacks
Router Attacks	Snooping or sniffing, message replay, message alteration, message delay and denial, address masquerading and spoofing, redirect, strict and loose routing, hijacking

Security and Tunneling Options as Cost Drivers of Using the Internet as an Extranet

Nevertheless, using the Internet as an extranet does in fact increase security costs in the sense that tunneling hardware and software is required to implement the Internet as an extranet in a secure fashion. This means that tools must be purchased to enable the creation of secure tunnels across the Internet. This usually involves purchasing a tunneling product or tools to authenticate users, set up the tunnel between specific Internet Protocol addresses, and to encrypt the data as it travels across the tunnel, and possibly to encrypt the data again when it is placed in storage.

Authentication of users and addresses is likely to require use of address pools or some other solution when employees and users of the Internet as an extranet travel a great deal and roam about the globe using and switching between various Internet Service Providers. Nevertheless, using the Internet as an extranet instead of using a proprietary solution like private-leased lines for communication across the enterprise is likely to be the less expensive solution because of the fierce competition between providers of open or nonproprietary network solutions.

In addition, the cost of securing the Internet as an extranet needs to be balanced against the benefits of and need for different tunneling options. For example, if the Internet is to be used only as a way for employees to send outgoing notices via Internet e-mail to suppliers then not much security is needed and secure tunnels are not required resulting in a less expensive, less complex, and widely available Internet as an extranet solution.

If, on the other hand, secure two-way data communication between distant business units is desired then compulsory tunnels are required; and secure tunnels will need to be required from network access servers. This solution will be more complex and expensive than the previous one. However, this solution will provide secure data communications between remote business units from firewall to firewall and without any breach of firewall security.

In effect, clients connect to a network access server which connects to a tunnel server which sets up and later breaks down the necessary tunnels. Although tunnel servers are required modifications, clients are not. In addition, compulsory tunneling is especially adapted to use of very thin clients because the tunnel servers take care of all of the tunnel setup, tear down, and security issues.

If secure data communication between remote and roaming employees is desired then voluntary tunnels are required. This solution will be more expensive and complex than the previous two. Firewall policy and packet filtering rules based upon source and destination addresses will become challenging. In addition, remote users will want to download applications through the firewall and across the tunnel, disconnect, run the application, and reconnect through the firewall and across a tunnel to upload the results of running the application. Firewalls flexible enough to limit application access to certain times of the day or from specified address pools may need to be purchased. In addition, roaming employees making use of voluntary tunnels may wish to connect to the Internet or to a printer while still connected through a voluntary tunnel to a client or application at the other end of the tunnel. Thus dynamic instead of static tunnels will be required. Although voluntary tunnels are dynamic, flexible, and capable of being widely deployed they do increase cost because every client must be equipped to do tunneling. In effect, clients become slightly fatter because they must include the functionality needed to set up, secure, and tear down voluntary tunnels.

Tunneling standards are still under development although rapid progress is being made.

Thus there are still differences in vendor implementations of protocol standards like remote dial-in user services and the EAP standard for token cards. This implies that in the short term some form of vendor lock in is likely for early implementors of tunneling. However, this situation is likely to change rapidly as standards become better defined and widely implemented in products. (Token cards are similar to personal identification numbers in that they are something that a user has to have in order to access a secured device or network.)

Regardless of what tunneling solution is adopted it will be important that security not be entirely dependent upon a possible single point of failure like a tunnel or a firewall. Thus, multiple firewalls, subnets, and multiple routers are required. Just like ancient castles used to have moats as well as multiple walls around them to guarantee their security your own security architecture and plan needs to include multiple defenses.

Security Management and Administration as Cost Drivers of Using the Internet as an Extranet

Regardless of which of these solutions is adopted and deployed, there will also be a need to manage remote systems through the firewall and across tunnels. Thus, firewalls flexible enough to permit SNMP (simple network management protocol) traps and system status reports to pass must be purchased. Voluntary or wormhole tunnels may also be required in order to enable remote system management and administration so that management and administration information can tunnel through the firewall at specific times via a voluntary or wormhole tunnel that exists only when it is needed.

Security, Application Gateways, and Application Programming Interfaces as Cost Drivers of Using the Internet as an Extranet

Achieving a high level of security over the Internet as an extranet will require the purchase and implementation of application gateways that restrict access to applications to specific times of the day and to specific trusted users. In addition, proxy servers that function as servers to those inside the firewall and clients to those outside will also be required along with implementation of application programming interfaces. All of these elements—application gateways, proxy servers, and application programming interfaces—will be described in greater detail in subsequent sections and chapters.

Use of application programming interfaces can increase security and lower costs for all of the following reasons.

▶ Application programming interfaces increase portability of solutions across operating systems because they have similar language bindings across operating systems.

▶ Application programming interfaces increase transparency by hiding implementation details from programmers and developers.

▶ Application programming interfaces increase modularity by ensuring that security programs are accessed through a limited number of function calls that can be replaced if a new application programming interface is adopted. Thus use of application programming interfaces represents at least a partial solution to scalability problems.

▶ Use of the same application programming interface by different programs increases the compatibility between different programs.

▶ Use of application programming interfaces increases maintainability because of the isolation of interface logic from business and data logic and because of the application programming interface limit on function calls.

▶ Application programming interfaces tend to last for a long time and can continue to be used even after new and improved versions are released.

Performance as a Cost Driver of Using the Internet as an Extranet

Many firewalls operate in promiscuous mode, meaning that they must examine every packet that passes them and make a decision about whether or not to allow the packet to pass through the firewall. This means that firewalls can easily become high-performance bottlenecks. This is especially likely to be a problem for big, fast networks emerging in large enterprises as extranets. Many firewalls saturate quickly as they try to examine every packet on 10 to 100 megabit networks. Thus fast, very high performance, and very reliable hardware and software may need to be purchased to make security and tunneling a practical reality for big fast networks. At the Spring 1997 Networld/Interop several Digital Alpha solutions with high-performance firewall software were described.

Web-enabled Application Development Cost Drivers of Using the Internet as an Extranet

One of the strongest reasons for designing, developing, deploying, and maintaining things like intranets and extranets is to enable the development, deployment, and maintenance of web-enabled enterprise applications similar to the FedEx example described below. The Internet as an extranet is a key enabling technology for these applications.

Thus, the cost and complexity of using the Internet as an extranet is closely tied to the cost and complexity of designing, developing, deploying, and maintaining, high-performance, mission-critical, enterprise-wide, web-enabled applications. The cost and complexity of designing, developing, deploying, and maintaining such applications can be viewed as closely related to or even an element of the cost of designing, developing, deploying, and maintaining the Internet as an extranet.

Although common gateway interface (CGI) programs are the least complex and expensive way to connect web servers to applications because they are based on writing scripts, they are not necessarily the best way to develop web-enabled applications. This is because common gateway interfaces are designed to connect to a database or back end application, get data, and return the data to the web server which returns the data to a browser. Thus the common gateway interface is a strictly sequential mode of requesting data that is extremely resource intensive because each request for data from a browser generates another connect and disconnect from the back end database or application engine. The common gateway interface may be inexpensive in terms of programmers' time but is extremely expensive in terms of hardware and software resources consumed. Use of common gateway interface to develop enterprise-wide, web-enabled applications can lead to user frustration with poorly performing applications.

There are several ways around this problem. Namely, use of ISAPI (Internet server application programming interface), WSAPI (web server application programming interface), or Java (both the Hot Java architecture and the Java programming interface). When combined with ODBC (open database connect) or JDBC (Java database connect) standards, programs written to the WSAPI, ISAPI, or Java application programming interfaces begin to overcome some of the limitations of the connect, get data, disconnect model implemented by the common gateway interface. The concurrency and multithreading options available by using these newer interfaces greatly lower the amount of hardware and software resources consumed in getting and returning data to web servers and browsers.

Although the newer interfaces greatly increase the performance of web-enabled applications by permitting concurrent connections to databases and caching of data, actually developing web-enabled applications using these interfaces requires expensive staff highly skilled in development of distributed client server solutions. In addition, the development and deployment of such systems requires management of database replication services and of concurrent connections and threads. Such complex systems are frequently both hard and expensive to develop.

The discussion in the above two or three paragraphs means that there is a classic economic trade-off decision to be made in the development and deployment of web-enabled applications. Namely, a choice has to be made between developing low-performance, web-enabled applications in an inexpensive and straight forward manner vs. developing high-performance, web-enabled applications in a more expensive and complex manner.

In spite of the cost and complexity involved, many businesses are today deciding to develop high-performance, enterprise-wide, web-enabled applications using the newer interfaces and tools described above. The cost and complexity of doing this is being minimized through architectures and implementations that make use of the concept of shared application services.

I can best explain what this concept means through an example. Suppose that like FedEx and some other companies you want to develop a web front end to your order management, credit check, and scheduling/shipping applications. In other words, you would like external customers to be able to go to your web site to find the current status of their shipment and location of their package. In addition, you would like your employees to click on the same web site to gain more detailed status on shipments and locations of packages. In addition, you would like customers to be able to place orders via your web server with or without the assistance of one of your employees. How can you best architect, develop, deploy, and maintain a system that does this?

An answer is by using shared application services. In other words, you design a single interface standard to your mission critical back end applications. Thus, whenever a web server wishes to query a mission critical application like order processing, credit check, or scheduling/shipping it does so via one standard application programming interface. This means that whenever a mission critical back end application changes only the interface and not all of the web servers or other applications need to be changed. This single point of change dramatically lowers the cost and complexity of developing, deploying, and managing web-enabled, mission-critical applications.

Benefits of Using the Internet as an Extranet

In addition to lower cost of networking by riding on the back of the Internet wide area infrastructure, use of the Internet as an extranet generates a number of business benefits. One benefit that is often missed in conversations and literature is that tying the organization together and enabling more transactions and user to user communication often increases awareness of the business rules being used in different parts of the organization. Understanding and managing business rules intelligently can dramatically improve business efficiencies. It is true that these results can be achieved with proprietary networks but only at higher cost and greater complexity of networking.

Another benefit of using the Internet as an extranet and of voluntary and compulsory tunneling is that it enables people to work at home and to connect to their employers while traveling. According to the figures mentioned at the Client Server World Conference in Boston in the spring of 1997, in 1996, 36% of U.S. homes contained a PC, 9% of European homes contained a PC, and 9% of Asian homes contained a PC. In 1997, the figure for U.S. homes is expected to increase to 38%. This is almost exactly the percentage of U.S. homes that can be expected to afford a $3,000 to $4,000 PC. However, as the price of PCs falls more and more homes can afford them and can be expected to purchase them. Even if only a small percentage of these PCs are used by people working at home then millions of workers will need access to data and applications within enterprises. In addition to people working at home, workers who travel as part of their jobs will also need access to data and applications within the enterprise. Tunnels and the Internet as an extranet network make this access possible.

It is important to remember that cost is not always the driving issue as companies decide whether or not to use the Internet as an extranet. Sometimes the need to address what the competition has done is a bigger issue. Ever since Charles Schwab developed a web site for customers and traders and FedEx developed a web site that customers can query to find out the status of their shipments, enterprises have rushed to develop extranets and Internets as virtual private networks regardless of the cost. Companies are rushing to develop web-enabled applications right now in spite of the technology challenges involved because of the enormous competitive advantages that such web-enabled applications offer their owners.

Cost is also less of an issue in some industries than others. For example, there are few high tech or information technology companies who can tolerate not having an extranet today.

Using the Internet for advertising, customer and supplier communications, and for transactions is rapidly becoming a mandatory business requirement for such firms. Having to build extranets and intranets puts these companies well along the path to using the Internet as a virtual private network. For not that much more expense, these companies can implement tunneling functions. In addition, portable net PCs are likely to drive down client-related cost of tunneling, which will be required to make mobile workers productive and competitive as they travel.

Templates and Tools for Cost and Benefits Estimates and Return on Investment Analyses

The following tables are meant to be templates or tools that you can modify to fit your own business and technology environments to perform your own return on investment calculations. These tools and templates are based upon my own research of web sites and summarize multiple discussions of the costs and benefits of deploying intranets, extranets, and tunneling or all of the elements of using the Internet as a virtual private network. Based upon the previous discussion of cost drivers and benefits you should feel comfortable modifying and filling out these tables.

Table 2.6 *A Summary of Initial Cost Estimates for Various Tunneling Options*

		Tunneling Options	
Initial	*No Tunnel*	*Compulsory Tunnel*	*Voluntary Tunnel*
Cost		Network Access Server	Access from Client
Element			
Estimates			
1. Client Setup			
TCP/IP Stack			

Table 2.6 *A Summary of Initial Cost Estimates for Various Tunneling Options (Continued)*

1. Client Setup (Continued)		
Winsock, etc.		
Licensing		
Installation		
2. Browsers		
Evaluation		
Licensing		
Installation		
Integration		
Plug-ins		
3. Platforms (new and upgrades)		
Memory and processor		
Disk Drives		
Operating System		
Windows 3.1		
Windows 95		
Office 97		
Other		
4. Web Server		
Setup		
Web server software		
Licensing		
Installation		
SMTP gateway for Internet e-mail		
Proxy server		
News server		
Search engines		

Table 2.6 *A Summary of Initial Cost Estimates for Various Tunneling Options (Continued)*

4. Web Server (Continued)		
Database access		
Log analyzers		
5. Security and Firewall		
Setup		
Firewall software		
Packet filters		
Licensing		
Installation		
Digital certificates		
6. Additional Software		
Authoring tools		
Conversion tools		
HTML editing tools		
Graphics tools		
Site managers		
7. Web-enabled		
Application		
Development Tools		
Common Gateway		
Interface		
Web API		
ISAPI		
Java		
Java Developers		
Kit		

Table 2.6 *A Summary of Initial Cost Estimates for Various Tunneling Options (Continued)*

7. Web-enabled (Continued)		
JDBC/ODBC		
8. Tunneling		
Software		
Licensing		
Installation		

Table 2.7 *A Summary of Ongoing Cost Estimates for Various Tunneling Options*

	Tunneling Options		
Ongoing	*No Tunnel*	*Compulsory Tunnel*	*Voluntary Tunnel*
Cost		*Network Access Server*	*Access from Client*
Element			
Estimates			
1. Personnel			
Costs			
Training			
Browser/search/retrieval			
Web-enabled application development specific			
Content provider personnel			
Help desk personnel			
Web masters			
Web managers			

Table 2.7 *A Summary of Ongoing Cost Estimates for Various Tunneling Options (Continued)*

2. Content		
Maintenance Costs		
Hours per file or per page		
Files or pages per week		
3. Management and Support Costs		
Browser administration		
Server administration		
Web masters		
Web managers		
Help desk support		

Related cost issues: subnets, proxy servers, dual homed hosts, nonrepudiation, and especially development of four tier client server solutions, etc.

Example Extranet Costs and Revenues

I highly recommend James Taschek's article, "Taking the Internet Private" (Jan. 1998) for the latest numbers on the costs and capabilities of extranet products. Extranet products include software for virtual private networks like Aventail, V-One, and AltaVista; hardware virtual private networks like products from Intel, Isolation Systems, RedCreek, Timestep, and VP Net; virtual private network-enabled firewalls from Raptor and Trusted Information Systems; and hardware firewalls from Watchguard. The client to server products range in price from $995 for a server + 10 clients and $89 for each additional client for 512 tunnels and an unlimited number of nodes supported to $5,495 per server + $80 per client for 200 tunnels and 5,000+ nodes supported. The server to server or LAN to LAN products range in price from $1,299 for 60 tunnels and an unlimited number of nodes supported to $11,995 for an unlimited number of tunnels and nodes supported.

Table 2.8 *A Summary of Internet as an Extranet Benefits*

	Type of Benefit	Source of Benefit	Initial $ Est.	Ongoing $ Est.
Tunneling				
Options				
1. No tunnel/ Internet Only	Inexpensive Easy to use Available to all	Standard components Not complex Widely accessible No breach of fire-wall policy		
2. Compulsory Tunnel/ Network Access Server	Encryption Authentication Address Setup at the NAS (Net-work Access Server)	Limited end to end transmission security No breach of fire-wall policy		
3. Voluntary Tunnel/Client-Based Access	Encryption Authentication Address Setup End to End	Maximum end to end transmission security Intentional breach of firewall policy		

Estimated Return on Investment =

Total business benefit of the new technology in $ divided by the total cost of the new technology in $.

As you can see, price clearly depends upon the number of tunnels and nodes that you want to support and therefore the total cost of an extranet clearly depends on the size of that extranet. I strongly recommend the article entitled "Building the Ties That Bind" (Pallato, Jan. 1998) for a sense of who is demanding extranet service and why they want it. Marketing and customers are the ones most demanding external service in the Fortune 1000 companies interviewed, and 82% of the companies surveyed are demanding external Internet services to exploit new business opportunities or respond to customer demand.

Extranets that enhance competitive advantage or enable new businesses can be sources of large revenues and therefore generate large returns on extranet investments. For example, "Website Makeovers E-commerce: Four to Watch" (March 1998) describes four businesses that use Internet commerce and extranet technologies to dramatically increase revenues.

Dell Computer is now doing $3 million a day in sales over the Internet. E-Toys now offers 5,000 toys for sales over the Internet. Auto-By-Tel says that it will triple its Internet-derived revenues from 1996 to 1997, and E-trade, a deep discount stock broker which sees 60% of its trades executed over an extranet, saw revenues grow 177% from 1996 to 1997 or from $51.6 million to $142.7 million.

Total Home Entertainment, the largest wholesaler of videos, CDs, computer games, and books in the United Kingdom, has successfully implemented an extranet that has allowed it to expand its market to include small international outlets outside the UK. These new customers can dial in any time day or night, place an order, and receive a confirmation electronically. Customers now perceive Total Home Entertainment as a leading edge company because of its on-line ordering systems. The benefit of such a perception may be hard to quantify, but many businesses consider such a perception to be a blessing.

The major challenge of doing a return on investment analysis of extranet investments is likely to be keeping calculations and expectations reasonable. It is worth remembering that customers and business partners have thousands of web sites to choose from and that they are only likely to visit yours if your web site offers them substantial added value. E-trade does this by charging some of the lowest prices in the industry—eight dollars per transaction for an unlimited number of shares which is many times less than the industry average charge. Dell offers customers the ability to configure their orders on-line thereby minimizing mistakes and increasing customer satisfaction. Auto-By-Tel offers their online customers a low-cost, haggle-free shopping experience, and E-Toys offers its on-line customers the ability to shop or browse by category: child's age, developmental benefits of toys (e.g., gross motor skills, intellectual development, etc.), type of toy, and brand.

Chapter Summary

In this chapter, I discussed the technology issues and user needs driving the costs, benefits, and return on investment analysis of using the Internet as an extranet. Much of the discussion focused on the unique security needs of roaming employees and remote suppliers. Scalability, management, administration, performance, application development, enterprise, and tunneling issues were also discussed. Specific tools and templates were offered so that you can develop your own forecasts of costs and benefits and perform your own return on investment analysis.

In addition, I provided information on the range and scaling of costs associated with several extranet products and four examples of companies that are achieving impressive revenue growth with extranet technologies. These examples should give you a sense of the numbers involved in return on investment calculations for extranets.

In the next chapter, I'll continue to develop the security issues and solutions surrounding the use of the Internet as an extranet. I'll start by explaining in detail how different types of security attacks and solutions apply to TCP/IP protocol layers. I'll also have more to say about the important issue of perceived versus real security of the Internet as an extranet.

3

The Challenges of Using Extranets

Chapter Objectives

This chapter explores and defines some of the challenges and problems presently associated with using the Internet as a virtual private network or extranet. (The terms Internet as a virtual private network, virtual private network or VPN, and extranet are used as synonyms in this chapter and throughout this book.) Many of these problems are being solved as I write this and thus represent opportunities as well as challenges. The primary objective of this chapter is to describe and define these problems so that the solutions to them that are described later in this book can be clearly understood by the reader. At the end of this chapter, I'll comment on the use of demilitarized zones or DMZs, which solve many of the problems discussed here.

There are two kinds of illustrations used in this chapter. The boxes with text in them are brief summaries of the challenges and problems described in this chapter. The other illustrations are meant to be interesting and to suggest some of the issues and complexities discussed in this chapter in a more artistic and abstract way. An objective of this chapter is to offer the reader a little bit of fun and humor in addition to practical knowledge by using the art work in this chapter to entertain, amuse, and inform.

The problems or challenges described in this chapter include the:

▶ Access Problem

▶ Architecture Problem

▶ Standards Problem

▶ Fat Versus Thin Client Problem

▶ Fat Versus Thin Server Problem

▶ Programmer Productivity Problem

▶ Performance Problem

▶ Reliability Problem

▶ Scalability Problem

▶ Security Perception Problem

▶ Security Problem

▶ Firewall Problem

▶ Who Do You Trust and How Much Do You Trust Them Problem

▶ Commercial Transactions Problem

The problems described here are hurdles to overcome. They are not necessarily show stoppers. Those enterprises who are first to overcome or to solve them are likely to achieve substantial business and competitive advantages by using the Internet as a virtual private network and by implementing extranets faster than their competitors. In fact both the technology of extranets and the experience of actually implementing and using extranets are advancing rapidly, and I'm optimistic that the challenges and problems described in this chapter are well on their way to being solved.

The Access Problem

The first step to understanding the nature of the "access problem" (see Note 3.1) is to attempt to answer the question of "Access to what from where, when, and for whom?" To answer this question we need to consider the different types of users who wish to consume services and software over the network as well as the different types of work that users do. In this context, a "user" is anyone who wishes to receive or send information or software over the network.

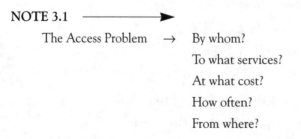

NOTE 3.1 ⟶

The Access Problem → By whom?

To what services?

At what cost?

How often?

From where?

It is interesting to note how the language used to describe users has shifted over time. In the past, great emphasis has been placed on the difference between "power users" and "casual users." The distinction between these two types of users often related to the number and types of applications run by each class of user.

Thus casual users ran one or two applications at most and seldom ran up against the bandwidth, speed, or memory limitations of the networks and computers that they used to get their jobs done. Power users on the other hand often pushed networks and machines to their bandwidth, speed, and memory limits as they ran multiple, heavy duty applications.

Casual users were often business administrators and managers who frequently used e-mail, word processing, spreadsheets, and little else. Power users were often engineers or scientists who frequently ran simulation, modeling, and heavy duty number crunching or graphical applications.

These two types of users needed access to very different types of applications at different times of the day from different locations. Casual users could be found wherever there were business offices during regular business hours. Power users were often found in laboratories and technical environments working late at night and running applications over the weekend. For the most part, both types of users accessed applications and information from fixed locations.

Somewhere between casual users and power users were systems operators or sysops and systems administrators or sysadmins who used networks and systems to create, manage, and delete accounts for end users of systems and networks, kept the network up and running whenever they were needed by the end user community, and who upgraded and managed the growth of networks and systems as the networks and systems grew. Often the sysops, sysadmins, and their closely related cousins or network managers (net managers) were tasked with managing security and protecting systems and networks from unauthorized intrusions and vandalism.

Although power users, casual users, sysops, sysadmins, and net managers continue to exist today, their need for access has dramatically changed in the last few years. The geographic mobility of many types of casual users has increased enormously and the size of networks that sysops, sysadmins, and net managers have to deal with has exploded. Many net managers now have to worry about extranets in addition to their internal networks. In addition, casual users sometimes evolve into power users as they learn to use more and more applications on their machines; thus, requiring not only geographic mobility but also high bandwidth and high speed access along with lots of memory on both clients and servers. Increasingly, everyone is becoming a power user in the sense of consuming greater bandwidth and network resources as they use networked applications like RealAudio, PointCast, or crunch huge spreadsheets.

Increasing numbers of workers who either work at home or who travel require access to data and applications not just 8 hours a day but 24 hours a day, 7 days a week, and 52 weeks a year. Geographically, mobile workers often try to access data and applications from remote time zones and at odd local times like the middle of the night or very early in the morning on a Sunday or holiday. This type of access often overwhelms modem pools and can create administrative and accounting nightmares if traveling end users try to connect to the company network using different Internet Service Providers with different billing and accounting requirements.

The Roaming Problem refers to the business, administrative, and technical challenges created by mobile employees who often switch Internet Service Providers. The Roaming Problem also creates some interesting network and system security challenges that are described below in the section on security.

In addition to the access challenges created by mobile users, the dramatic growth in the size and distributed nature of many computer systems and networks has made it difficult and expensive for net managers and sysops to administer and manage machines by physically touching or visiting them. Instead, there is a huge need for remote system management using computer networks. For example, if upgrading a PC with new software requires someone to sit in front of the machine, insert diskettes, and run an install program and there are thousands of PCs requiring the upgrade then upgrading all of the PCs will be extremely expensive and time consuming even if an operator only requires 45 minutes in front of each PC! Many software upgrades actually require more than 45 minutes in front of the machine in order to implement them.

Thus, there is enormous economic and business incentive to ship and install software upgrades from one server to many PCs or other clients so that no human being has to go sit in front of each client! The same economic and business incentives apply to most of the other functions that net managers, sysops, and sysadmins perform as well. The net managers, sysops, and sysadmins may require 24 hours a day, 7 days a week, and 52 weeks a year access to every device on the network.

In addition to their need for local access in order to carry out their administrative and management tasks, the net managers, sysops, and sysadmins often need access to remote devices in order to run tools on them. For example, net managers often run tools like trace route that reports the exact route that packets of information take as they cross the Internet and ping or loop back that sends packets to a specific destination machine which verifies its presence on the network by sending the same or different packets back to the sending machine.

Net managers, sysops, and sysadmins frequently use tools to jump from host to host, add and delete accounts, and to manage passwords in order to add or delete both people and machines from the network. They frequently use tools and programs like telnet to reach remote hosts, login and set user identification to control host access, utilities like file transfer protocol to move files around the network, and other tools to probe remote hosts. Effective use of these tools requires access to remote network resources. Thus like some of their more mobile business colleagues, net managers, sysops, and sysadmins sometimes require frequent, high bandwidth, and high-speed access to remote applications, data, and machines.

Because part of their job function is to keep the computer network up and running, security is a concern of net managers, sysops, sysadmins or technical managers. A key element of protecting networks from security attacks is to run log and audit files on remote machines. Technical managers need the network and system access to run the log and audit programs 24 hours a day, 7 days a week, and 52 weeks a year in order to protect their networks and computers from hackers or, more accurately, crackers.

The original meaning of the term "hacker" was complimentary and meant someone knowledgeable enough and skilled enough to know a way around tough computer problems. Today, the term "hacker" has become confused with the term "cracker" which refers to someone who intentionally violates computer and network security for their own ends. Chasing and catching crackers frequently requires a lot of remote access.

The answer to the questions of "Access to what?"; "Access from where?"; and "Access when?" often depends on the nature of the work to be done by users of the network as well as their interests and personalities. Thus different categories of users require access to different types of data and applications. For example, sales reps often need remote access to order management, credit check, and shipping/dispatch applications and price files. Field service reps often need remote access to parts lists and field service manuals at any time day or night. Casual users may be satisfied with remote access to e-mail and an expense reimbursement application, but power users may well demand remote access to sophisticated simulation and modeling tools. Net managers, sysops, and sysadmins are very likely to want remote access to everything on the network any time day or night in addition to a large tool chest of system and network diagnostic, test, and fix tools and patches.

Some types of users are more patient than others when it comes to accepting some "reasonable" limitations on unrestricted access. For example, casual users and business managers are likely to be very impatient with access schemes that require them to remember and to enter multiple passwords to access their client machine, a network server, an application server, and possibly even a database server. When faced with requests to set or choose multiple passwords, some users choose the same password for everything so that they will not have trouble remembering it.

Even users as technical as net managers, sysops, and sysadmins (hereafter referred to as technical managers) sometimes become so impatient with requirements to enter multiple passwords to gain access that they implement workarounds or create accounts that do not require passwords for access so that they will not have to enter multiple passwords every time that they need access to a remote network or system resource. This may be bad practice, but is understandable if the technical user has to access many remote accounts to do their job. The technical users are likely to be only a little more patient than the casual users when it comes to entering multiple passwords to gain access to remote applications, data, and machines.

Another piece of the access challenge is the question of "Access by what type of client to what type of server?" Some companies have chosen for business and technical reasons to standardize on certain types of client environments. Thus they may allow access to certain applications by PCs and not Macs or vice versa. Other companies are placing browsers on every client in order to attempt to achieve platform independence at least at the client level.

Other companies have decided that low-speed access is a good way to keep access costs down while providing casual users with sufficient access to do their jobs. Yet other companies are willing to pay for high-speed dedicated lines so that they can provide access to audio and video data by their employees.

Availability and reliability of access can be a contentious issue especially for roaming or traveling users who often try to reach the home offices through a variety of Internet Service Providers as they travel around the globe. Availability and reliability of access is definitely not the same in every location. For example, in parts of Africa there is no Internet access because there is no network or telecommunications infrastructure in place to support access. Even in the Americas access can be easier and more reliable or harder and less reliable at certain times of the day.

Likewise, access costs can vary significantly from location to location. Some ISPs offer local services with local telephone numbers and a more expensive service with 800 numbers for customers who frequently travel. Some ISPs offer only Internet access while others offer additional information services that they charge for in addition to access.

The Architecture Problem

The architecture challenge for VPNs or extranets depends very much on the nature of the work to be done over the network (see Note 3.2). For example, if end users do much of their work in an off-line or standalone fashion and connect to the Internet to send their work product over the wires to corporate headquarters, they may strongly prefer an architectural approach that recognizes their need for fully functional PCs and fat clients. Some reporters and writers are an examples of this type of worker.

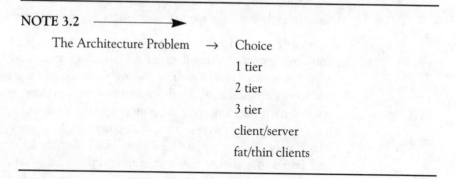

NOTE 3.2

The Architecture Problem → Choice

1 tier

2 tier

3 tier

client/server

fat/thin clients

Sales reps on the other hand may wish to use the extranet to do nothing more than to place orders and check on the status of orders and prices. In other words, if they use computers at all, they use them on-line only. Thus, sales reps may be quite happy with an architectural approach that recognizes their need for thin clients only. Moreover, if the sales reps travel a lot and have to carry their client box with them, they may prefer the light weight of a thin client over the heavier weight of a fat client especially if the sales reps do not need access to standard applications that imply significant weight to the client box.

NOTE 3.3 ——————————▶

    The fat vs. thin client debate   → Standalone vs. on-line work

    Or how friendly is the net anyway?   ← Nature of the work?

The architectural choice between deploying fat versus thin clients or net PCs which are programmable thin clients is likely to be gray and not black and white (see Note 3.3). This is because fat and thin client technology is evolving rapidly and instead of two choices only for clients there is likely to be a whole range of client devices ranging from the very thin and inexpensive to the very fat and expensive. Different types of workers are likely to require different types of clients depending upon the nature of their work.

Most new systems currently under development follow some form of client server-distributed computing architecture. This is largely because of the widespread preference for adaptive design. The beauty of adaptive systems is that as the business and technical environment changes adaptive systems can easily change with them. Thus, adaptive systems make heavy use of components or modules with standard communication interfaces so that modules can be reused or swapped in and out as needed. In addition, the use of modules with standard communication interfaces lessens dependence on any single vendor's module and fosters competition between vendors.

Adaptive systems tend to separate presentation logic, business logic, and data into separate modules or groups of modules. In other words, adaptive systems tend to follow the architecture and logic of multi-tier client server architecture. Many companies are developing web-based front ends to their mission-critical business applications. In these architectures, a client contacts a web server which then contacts an application server which may contact a data base server in order to deliver an application and data to the client. The web front end provides a common interface for accessing mission-critical applications. This standard or common interface makes it easier for users to use and learn new applications and standardizes the application presentation to the end user.

Some authors believe that these architectures are evolving in the direction of thin clients and fat servers running most of the application and business logic and doing the database access. In fact, a sort of componentization of server functionality may be occurring with reusable server modules being developed. Perhaps these modules or components will eventually be marketed much as plug-ins or client components are marketed today.

Choices between fat and thin clients, fat and thin servers, adaptive systems, components, standard communication protocols and interfaces, and 1 to n tier client server designs are some of the major architectural choices and challenges to be made when developing a VPN of extranet. The adaptive system concept and popularity of Internet protocols like http and TCP/IP are important architectural principles to keep in mind.

Perhaps one of the biggest architectural commercial battles now occurring is between standards like Common Object Request Broker, Distributed Component Object Method, and Java. These are communication protocols for communication between distributed objects and to some extent represent competitive battles between Sun Microsystems, Microsoft, and others. They are likely to be around for some time to come and represent the kinds of communication standards that make adaptive systems possible. I'll have more to say about objects and their relationship VPNs later.

Here's the bottom line: the architectural challenge in developing an extranet or VPN is largely one of choosing the right technologies and standards in order to develop adaptive systems which can be easily and inexpensively modified as business and technical requirements change.

The Standards Problem

The challenge of choosing the right set of standards to follow is closely related to two things; namely, the architecture that you choose to implement and your choice of a vendor or vendors that you can and must rely upon (see Note 3.4). This is because different architectural implementations require different standards and because vendors race to implement open standards while at the same time adding proprietary extensions to the standards in order to create more competitive and functional products. The proprietary extensions offer consumers better products but only at the risk of vendor lock-in.

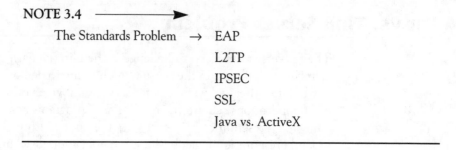

NOTE 3.4

The Standards Problem	→	EAP
		L2TP
		IPSEC
		SSL
		Java vs. ActiveX

Most of the standards that surround VPNs involve either tunneling protocols or security and encryption protocols. Thus L2TP is a tunneling protocol from Microsoft. EAP is a security standard defining token cards and their use. IPSEC is an Internet Protocol security standard. SSL is the secure sockets layer protocol. There are many many more protocols especially around ActiveX, Java, and encryption that could be mentioned. You can expect to see many vendor wars and competitions roaring around competing protocol standards. However, the important point to remember as you contemplate the acronym soup of numerous protocol standards is that you need to choose those protocols that are consistent with your architectural choices and with some set of vendors that support your choice of protocol standards.

Fat vs. Thin Client Problem

As was hinted at above, the choice between deploying fat versus thin clients often involves balancing the needs of different end user communities. For example, sales reps may prefer very thin clients because they want to carry as light a client with them as possible as they travel from customer site to customer and because they usually do their work online in terms of placing orders, checking on availability of product, and checking on prices and credit worthiness. Writers and reporters on the other hand may prefer fat clients because they do much of their work off-line and use the network to ship files to headquarters only after their stories are written.

The previous chapter developed the cost issues and related discussions that surround thin versus fat clients and net PCs. The point made here is different. The point made here is that the choice between fat and thin clients is just as much a function of differing user needs and politics as it is a function of cost. Thus, part of the challenge represented by choosing between fat and thin clients is political rather than purely financial and technical.

Fat vs. Thin Server Problem

The fat versus thin server challenge is the mirror image of the fat versus thin client challenge in the sense that choosing to deploy thin clients usually requires the deployment of fat servers and vice versa. This is because most applications require the execution of programs against some type of data and presentation of results to the user. Although one can shift around presentation logic, business or application logic, and data between clients and servers, all of this logic and data must reside and run either on clients or on servers or on both for applications to run successfully. Thus, the challenge of choosing between fat and thin servers or a mixture of both involves all of the issues discussed above and in the previous chapter in the section on fat versus thin clients and net PCs.

The Programmer Productivity Problem

The programmer productivity challenge (see Note 3.5) is relevant to the development and deployment of extranets and VPNs because these types of networks are frequently developed and deployed in order to help distributed teams of programmers develop code faster and to help remote users gain access to local applications quickly and conveniently.

NOTE 3.5 ——————————▶

The Programmer Productivity Problem: No reusability

Code quality/maintainability

Complex languages

In fact, the programmer productivity challenge is much the same whether developing web-enabled applications or more traditional applications. With the exception of use dynamic link and load libraries and frameworks which are available from software vendors, there is still very little reusability of code by most software developers. Most application software develop remains more of an art or craft rather than a science with distressing implications for software quality and application maintainability.

In future chapters, we'll take a look at how a VPN can be used to move software development teams and efforts away from a cowboy style of software development and toward ways of developing software that are definable, repeatable, measurable, manageable, and may be even improvable. An extranet or VPN alone cannot guarantee a world-class software development effort with greater reusability of higher quality code modules, but it can help!

The Performance Problem

Lack of high performance at busy times of the business day is one of the reasons why some users consider the Internet and VPNs based on it to be unfriendly (see Note 3.6). Unfortunately, in too many localities the beginning or end of the East Coast and West Coast business day is not a good time to access and use the Internet.

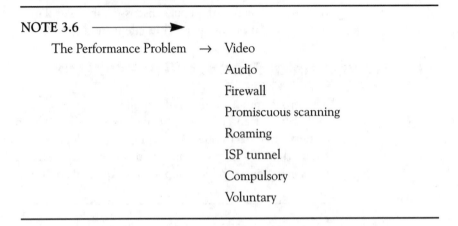

NOTE 3.6 ⟶

The Performance Problem → Video

Audio

Firewall

Promiscuous scanning

Roaming

ISP tunnel

Compulsory

Voluntary

The performance problem is far worse when it comes to moving audio or video data over the Internet. Too many users are still not equipped with the right software and tools to compress and decompress let alone encrypt or decrypt audio or video data sent over the Internet.

I know many Internet users who intentionally restrict their use of the Internet to the exchange of text only for exactly this reason. Moreover, many firewalls lack the high performance needed to examine and filter millions of audio and video packets of data streaming past them in real time. This is an area where faster hardware and software can help solve the performance problem.

The severity of the performance challenge also depends upon what type of tunneling is being used as well as upon what the user is doing with their tunnel. In the simplest of tunneling schemes which amounts to simply confining your data to a particular ISP network and never letting the data leave that ISP's network to travel to the broader Internet, performance is limited to the performance characteristics of the ISP's network itself.

In the more technically sophisticated compulsory tunneling schemes, performance depends upon the performance characteristics of the tunnel server that sets up and tears down the tunnel in addition to the performance characteristics of the network servers and network infrastructure used to support the tunnel. Performance is likely to vary most of all in the case of voluntary tunneling because software on clients at each end of the voluntary tunnel sets up and tears down the tunnel and because the voluntary tunnel depends heavily on the network servers and infrastructure used to communicate through the tunnel. Thus, the performance challenge depends upon many factors including what the user is trying to do, the type of tunnel, network, and ISP infrastructure.

The Reliability Problem

If you ask business executives why they are not in a bigger hurry to implement business transactions and mission-critical applications over the Internet, many of them will tell you that they have major concerns about the reliability and security of the Internet (see Note 3.7). Reliability of extranets has an immediate impact for better or worse on customers, suppliers, employees, and other business partners. When a transaction fails for whatever reason over the extranet this failure is often very visible to all sorts of business partners.

NOTE 3.7 ————————————▶

The Reliability Problem → Mission critical apps

Impacts business partners, customers, and staff

The concept of reliability includes the concepts of availability and freedom from errors.

In other words, many users regard a network as reliable only if it is available to them whenever they need it for as long as they need it and it operates without error while they need it. Given the geographically dispersed nature of users, diversity of client environments, the explosion of Internet traffic which often doubles every ten months, and the diverse needs of users establishing and maintaining high degrees of reliability can be quite a challenge indeed.

The Scalability Problem

The scalability challenge is closely related to the reliability challenge because of the rapid growth of the Internet (see Note 3.8). With both the volume of IP traffic and the number of users connecting to the Internet growing at a rate of 165% per year according to one 1995 Networld/ Interop presenter, ISPs and others have had their hands full assigning

TCP/IP addresses to new customers and helping their customers register with InterNIC and ISA who manage the assignment of Internet addresses and domain names and structures.

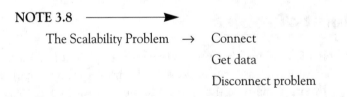

NOTE 3.8 ————————————▶

    The Scalability Problem   →   Connect

                                  Get data

                                  Disconnect problem

Most of the growth in IP traffic has come as a result of new users connecting up to the Internet and not as a result of increasing utilization of the Internet on the part of established users. However, this could change in the future as existing users develop greater appetites for audio and video data and applications that consume large amounts of network bandwidth.

As the ISPs attempt to route or move IP data from server to server and routing computer to routing computer across the multiple networks that make up the Internet, they have experienced explosive growth in the size and rate of change of routing tables that keep track of the frequently changing addresses of Internet users and of routing computers. As the ISPs seek to keep up with these changes, they are frequently unsure who to call at other networks to resolve questions of address changes and conflicts. Even the "Who Is?" program that keeps track of various networks, their network manager contact names, and telephone numbers has not kept up with the growth of the Internet.

ISPs are not the only ones challenged by the explosive growth of the Internet. Developers of web-enabled mission-critical business applications have also been challenged by Internet and extranet or VPN scalability issues. The traditional model of browsers connecting to web servers every time they need to get data and then disconnecting does not scale well as many users attempt to access the same data or run the same applications because in the traditional model each access, connect, and disconnect burdens the network with dedicated single user channels.

In future chapters, we'll explore the different solutions being used today to meet and resolve the scalability challenge. We'll discuss how additional TCP/IP addressing structure and delegation by ISA and InterNIC are helping ISPs solve their scalability problems. In addition, we'll look at software engineering techniques that help solve the dedicated single user channel problem.

The Security Perception Problem

The security perception challenge is probably the single greatest reason why the general consumer is not ready to embrace the Internet today for commercial transactions (see Note 3.9). Many consumers perceive the Internet as a world of hackers and information terrorists who can't wait to steal consumer's dollars, credit card numbers, and other business and personal information.

NOTE 3.9 ——————————▶

The perception problem   →   It's a world of hackers with unlimited risks!

The net is full of information terrorists!

Strangely enough, many consumers who would never send their credit card numbers over the Internet, don't hesitate to send their credit card numbers across the voice telephone system. In reality, the telephone system is probably no more or less secure than the Internet. However, the telephone system is certainly perceived by many consumers to be far more secure than the Internet.

The fact that, in this case, perception is not quite reality comes as a surprise to many people. For example, many people don't realize that if their credit card number is stolen while traveling over the Internet the same limits of personal financial liability apply as to the theft or loss of credit card numbers in any other way. This is usually consumer liability only for the first $50 of fraudulent purchases with the stolen credit card number.

In addition, many consumers don't realize that the greatest threat to the security of their credit card numbers comes from attempts to access and steal files of credit card numbers directly from credit card vendors rather than from attempts to grab the credit card numbers as they flow across the Internet.

Many consumers deny that they use the Internet for financial transactions because they define a "financial transaction" too narrowly as an exchange of cash or credit card numbers. These same consumers are, in fact, using the Internet and the web sites of major financial organizations to balance their stock portfolios and invest for retirement. These are some of the largest financial transactions of many consumers' life times!

Many consumers are unaware of the gigantic advances that have been made in encryption and other security technologies that if used properly can dramatically improve extranet security. We'll discuss this technology in future chapters and try to bring the perception of security a little closer to the potential reality of Internet and extranet security.

The Security Problem

The actual security challenge to implementing extranets or VPNs is significant and the subject of substantial research and development efforts with significant progress being made (see Note 3.10). Increasingly new security technology is becoming an enabler of electronic commerce over the Internet.

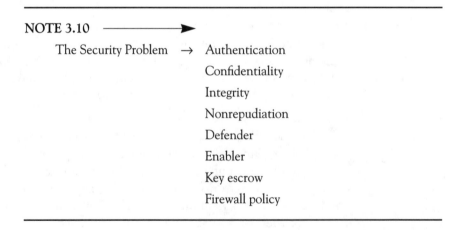

NOTE 3.10

The Security Problem   →   Authentication

Confidentiality

Integrity

Nonrepudiation

Defender

Enabler

Key escrow

Firewall policy

The security challenges that surround tunneling and extranets are in many respects similar to the security issues that surround networks in general. Thus, whenever a tunnel is created authentication of the user needs to occur, confidentiality of the information flowing through the tunnel needs to occur, and confidentiality of information has to be maintained after the information has flowed through the tunnel and been stored.

In addition, the receiver of the information will want to know that the information received is exactly the same as the information that was sent and that information actually came from the person or machine reputed to have sent it. Moreover, the sender will want to know that the receiver will not be able in the future to repudiate the information sent by claiming that some other message was originally sent. Thus, information integrity, nonrepudiation, and signature authentication are important parts of the extranet security challenge. (See Note 3.11.)

NOTE 3.11 ————————▶

The Message Problem   →   Who really wrote it?

Was the message changed?

Part of the challenge of implementing encryption technologies is key management issues. There are legal requirements dealing with the export of keys of various lengths and with the retrieval and escrow of the keys used to encrypt and decrypt information. We'll explore these issues and discuss how cryptology can be used to increase extranet security in future chapters.

Also, we'll take a look at managing and encrypting password files since access to and theft of these files is often the goal of hackers or any one who wants to breach extranet and intranet security. In addition, we'll take a brief look at how some network management tools can be used to both decrease and increase extranet security.

The Firewall Problem

Firewall policy is a significant security challenge when it comes to tunneling and implementation of extranets (see Note 3.12). For example, if the firewall does not decrypt all of the information tunneling through it then a voluntary tunnel can carry a virus right through the firewall to infect the entire enterprise network. If, on the other hand, the firewall does decrypt all the information passing through it and scan for viruses then the enterprise network is protected from viruses but employees maintaining the firewall may well have access to all extranet transmissions even e-mail between CEOs discussing potential mergers or other sensitive financial transactions.

NOTE 3.12 ————————▶

Firewalls are forever because you manage one thing instead of many things.

We'll discuss these and other firewall issues in future chapters. Also, we'll also take a look at the proposition that "firewalls are forever" in the sense that it is much easier for sysops, sysadmins, and net managers to manage a few firewalls than it is to manage and secure every client and server on the network.

The Who Do You Trust and When Do You Trust Them Problem

As we explore the challenges to developing and implementing extranets or VPNs, we'll find that solving these problems and meeting these challenges requires that intentional decisions be made about who to trust and how much to trust them (see Figure 3.1). We'll find that different levels of trust are required for different members of the extranet team whether they are suppliers, customers, employees, consultants, or machines. In future chapters, we'll explore the effects of these decisions on security policies, reliability, performance, scalability, access, and architecture.

The Commercial Transactions Problem

Payment and rewards for posting information to the world wide web has a large impact on what information actually gets posted to and shared or sold over an extranet (see Note 3.13). For example, the press recently reported that when one technical university asked its students to publish their undergraduate and graduate theses on the university extranet, the students refused because professional academic publications would not accept all or any part of material previously published elsewhere. This would severely limit the future job and promotion prospects of many stu-

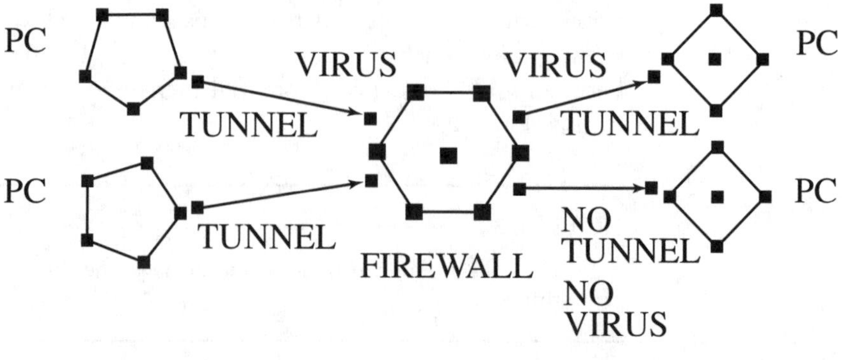

Figure 3.1
Who Do You Trust and How Much?

PC VIRUS VIRUS PC
TUNNEL TUNNEL
PC PC
TUNNEL NO
TUNNEL
FIREWALL NO
VIRUS

dents. The school responded to this challenge by asking students to make summaries or abstracts of their research available over the university extranet.

NOTE 3.13 ———————————➤

    The Commercial Transactions Problem   →   Rewards

                                                       Penalties

                                                       Alternatives

---

In future chapters, we'll look at the challenges and problems surrounding conducting commercial transactions over the extranet especially those challenges associated with sale of intellectual property over the extranet and with measuring and billing for the different types of products and intellectual property sold. We'll look at solutions to the commercial transactions problem from both a producer and consumer perspective.

So What's The Bottom Line Here

According John Pallato in his article, "Building the Ties That Bind," the next few years are likely to be a period of intense experimentation as companies install the currently available extranet products and bear the administrative burden and costs necessary to make extranets work.

I couldn't agree more, and I believe that this experimentation is well on its way to solving the problems discussed here. For example, today many companies implementing extranets are meeting their needs for security and ease of administration by implementing DMZs or demilitarized zones. DMZs are sub-networks that are separated from a business's core intranet and that can be securely accessed by remote users, business partners, and/ or customers. Two businesses that wish to communicate via an extranet can set up DMZs that talk to each other. Any breaches of security would affect only the DMZs and not the core intranets of the two businesses.

According to Forrester Research as cited in "Building the Ties That Bind" (Pallato, Jan. 1998), the DMZ era of extranet development will continue through the year 2000. More than 50% of the fifty Fortune 1000 companies surveyed by Forrester Research Group plan to use the Internet within two years to communicate with their business partners and 67% said that they plan to execute transactions with customers over the Internet.

Chapter Summary

This chapter has defined and explained many of the challenges of developing and implementing extranets especially those challenges and problems concerning the:

▶ Access Problem

▶ Architecture Problem

▶ Standards Problem

▶ Fat vs. Thin Client Problem

▶ Fat vs. Server Problem

▶ Programmer Productivity Problem

▶ Performance Problem

▶ Reliability Problem

▶ Scalability Problem

▶ Security Perception Problem

▶ Security Problem

▶ Firewall Problem

▶ Who Do You Trust and How Much Do You Trust Them Problem

▶ Commercial Transactions Problem

This chapter also indicated that the next two years of extranet design and implementation is likely to be a period of intense experimentation as companies test new products and the administration required to make extranets work. DMZs offer a near term solution to many of the problems discussed in this chapter especially the problems related to security.

Future chapters will further develop these problems and propose specific solutions to them. The aim will be to be both theoretical and practical so that readers can make progress in overcoming some of these challenges in implementing their own extranets.

4

Access Solutions for Extranets

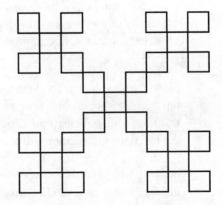

Chapter Objectives

The objectives of this chapter are to discuss and explore the following solutions to the problems of extranet access as defined in an earlier chapter. We discuss:

▶ The explosion occurring in Internet and extranet access.

▶ The reasons why people want remote access to the enterprise via an extranet and how they justify their need to management.

▶ The two primary types of remote access to the extranet. 1. Remote dial up access. 2. Extending the LAN to the small office home office via routers and bridges with Ethernet connections.

▶ Enterprise class solutions with multiple channels or connections per port.

▶ Management of access options in terms of automated ping, automated dial up, and automated build up and tear down of connections.

▶ Hybrid vs. dedicated hardware and software systems for remote access.

▶ Tunneling, bandwidth control, and security protocols such as L2FP, L2TP, PPTP, PAP, CHAP, MLP, MLP+, BACP, and IPSec.

▶ Different security paradigms such as what the user knows, what the user has, and unique user identifier systems for controlling and managing remote access.

▶ Synchronization of user lists on network access servers and home gateways.

▶ The business benefits and risks of remote access to the enterprise via the extranet.

▶ The challenges and solutions to remote access presented by going international or global including issues of personnel security, physical security of hardware and software, encryption/decryption laws, differing legal systems, and competitive environments.

▶ A case study.

Note that a solution to extranet access challenges and problems is a combination of several different elements including hardware, software, user training, and policies and procedures. All of these elements need to be deployed and implemented in order to approach anything like a complete solution. I'll end this chapter with a brief case study on Cisco Systems because I believe that Cisco Systems has made the most progress in solving the problems and challenges described in this chapter and is far along in designing and implementing a successful extranet.

The Explosion Occurring in Internet and Extranet Access

The following tables tell the story of the explosion currently occurring in Internet and extranet access and also give an indication of the growth of

Table 4.1 *The Growth of Electronic Commerce and Access to the Internet and Extranet*

Year	Business Results
2000	$100 billion in revenues flowing across the Internet and extranets
Expected Values	100 million customers on line
	1 million corporations transacting business over the Internet and extranet
	50% of all transactions occur overseas
	70% of all transactions on the Internet involve companies with fewer than 100 employees

Table 4.1 *The Growth of Electronic Commerce and Access to the Internet and Extranet (Coninued)*

Year	Business Results
1996	$100 million in revenues flowed across the Internet and extranets
Actual Values	35 million customers on line
	190 thousand companies conducted business over the Internet or extranet
	77% of all transactions occurred within the United States
	33% of all transactions on the Internet involve companies with fewer than 100 employees

(Data based upon several Spring 1997 Networld + Interop discussions and public presentations.)

Table 4.2 *Individual Case Studies*

Company	Results
Amazon.com	Revenues increasing 100% per quarter from a base of $16 million in the winter of 1996.
	An enormous cash success story because electronic payments for books are received within 24 hours of the order being placed, but bills are not paid until day 40 or so.
	Revenue per employee is three times better than the average revenue per employee for a super store. In 1996 revenue per employee at Amazon.com was $300,000 or three times better than for the average super bookstore.
Cisco	Doing $5 million per day over the Internet.
	Increases in customer loyalty and satisfaction through the use of configuration agent, pricing agent, and status agent. Customer queries to the web replaced 74,000 customer telephone calls per week.
	No customized pricing as yet.
Dell Computer	Doing $1 million per day in revenue over the Internet in 1996.
Charles Schwab	Expected to do $500 to $750 million in financial transactions over the Internet in 1996.
GE	Expected to do $500 to $750 million in transactions over its extranet (GEIS) in 1996.

(Data based on several Spring 1997 Netowrld + Interop public presentations.)

electronic commerce over the net. Much of the data in these tables comes from public presentations and conversations at industry conferences like Networld + Interop Spring 1997 and DCI Client Server World Spring 1997, Software Productivity Group conferences, and others.

Table 4.3 *Players Who Compete to Provide Internet Access and Their Strengths*

Type of Company	Strength as an Access Provider
Telecommunications	These companies have access to almost every home and business in the United States through their telephone wires.
Cable Co.	These companies own cables that can bring high bandwidth to the home.
Internet Service Provider	These companies provide nimble, creative, and inexpensive Internet access.

Table 4.4 *A Phased Approach to Allowing Customer Access to Financial Services Web Sites*

Step #
1. Permit customers to access ads on your web server.
2. Permit customers to look up their own account information and detail on your web server.
3. Permit customers to do financial transactions with your web server.
Web applications often follow voice or voice mail applications in terms of their phases of development.

Table 4.5 *Buying Patterns for Web-Based Mission-Critical Solutions*

1. Customer budgets are often negotiated and determined from July to October.
2. Prices for voice mail applications often compete with prices for web-based data applications.
3. Many customers believe that by adopting open, standards-based network architectures they can lower their overall cost of ownership by 5 to 10 times. (Perhaps from a $25,000 monthly cost of running a proprietary network to a $6,000 monthly cost for running an open, standards-based network.)

Table 4.6 *Extranet Advantages from a Consumer and/or Merchant Perspective*

1.	Overcomes limitations or boundaries of space and time.
2.	Allows the merchant to provide the customer with a complete history of customer transactions.
3.	Allows customers to complete templates describing their interests and to receive news and information on products and services that match their interests via push technologies.
4.	Allows the merchant to use collaborative filtering to gather information on and to build customer profiles without this being known by the customer.
5.	A steady improvement in emulation and simulation from emulating the United States Post Office with text-based e-mail to emulating a game of golf with virtual reality.

Several large multinational companies and their intranet and extranet managers, use the following "back of the envelope" calculation to forecast the number of accesses across an intranet or extranet to an application. Although the method is informal, it is worth knowing and modifying to fit your own business and technical environment. The reasoning or calculation goes as follows:

1. Of the total number of world wide enterprise employees and business partner employees (say 30,000 in this case) how many of them have browsers? Let's say 20,000 of them do.

2. Of the total number of enterprise and business partner employees with browsers, how many of them are on line at any given time? Perhaps 2/3 if the employees and browsers are evenly distributed across the globe. Let's say 12,700 in this case.

3. Of the total number of enterprise and business partner employees who have browsers and who are likely to be on line at any given point in time, how many of them are likely to attempt to access the application in question at approximately the same time? Perhaps one or two percent in this case or 150–300 users.

This type of calculation is useful because it can give a rough or preliminary sizing of an extranet access challenge. Preliminary sizing estimates are often useful in testing vendor claims and in understanding business justifications for proposed projects and purchases. The result of the calculation can be used to prototype and test extranet access solutions. The solutions can then be piloted and the true size of the extranet access challenge along with the proposed solutions can be tested and verified.

Table 4.7 *Economic Impact of Extranets*

▶ Disintermediation or replacement of the "middleman."

▶ A search for competitive differentiation and added value on the part of surviving "middlemen."

▶ A convergence of the education, data, and entertainment industries.

▶ There is a need for business to business as well for business to consumer web-based solutions.

Table 4.8 *The Infrastructure Challenge to the Growth of Global Extranets*

Country	Number of Telephone Main Lines per 100 People
1. Argentina	14
2. Belgium	45
3. Brazil	7
4. Canada	58
5. Chile	11
6. Czech Republic	21
7. China	2
8. Egypt	4
9. France	55
10. Germany	48
11. Iraq	3
12. Mexico	9
13. Russia	16
14. Singapore	47
15. Thailand	4
16. United States	59

Telephone Main Lines per 100 People for Selected Countries (Taken from the *Statistical Abstract of the United States 1996*, numbers for 1994.)

The point of including this last table is to illustrate the wide range of telephone lines and telecommunications infrastructure in different countries of the world. In some countries, network infrastructure is readily available and in other countries it is not. This diversity of the availability of telecommunications infrastructure is a major challenge to the design and implementation of extranets that span the globe.

Solutions to the global infrastructure challenge to the growth of extranets are use of global 800 numbers, call back or automatic dial back, and use of satellite links as long distance carriers in parts of Asia and Africa. In addition to the shear lack of infrastructure, the fact that many post offices and telephone companies are government-backed monopolies in many foreign countries increases the prices of services and makes the supplier of telecommunication infrastructure services less responsive.

Since there are relatively low barriers to entry to the Internet Service Provider business today, we can look forward to a fairly quick closing of the infrastructure gap across the globe. In fact, those parts of the globe with little or no infrastructure but with money can probably skip over some of the older technology and implement the newer technologies today. This should accelerate the growth of the global ISP business that is already growing faster than the original PC business.

Why Users and Management Want Remote Access

According to figures mentioned at the Spring 1997 Networld + Interop, 55 million people will be telecommuting to work in the United States by the year 2000. The figure mentioned for 1997 was about 15 million people. These figures are a strong statement about the growth of and preference for telecommuting in the United States. Clearly, many people would rather telecommute to work than drive down the highway to work and apparently many employers agree.

There are many personal and business reasons why workers prefer to connect electronically to their work place rather than in person. People who live and work in areas of high traffic density often prefer to telecommute during the morning rush hour and to drive to their corporate office later in the day when the traffic is less severe. Some people feel that this practice of telecommuting in the morning and coming into work later increases their personal productivity. In fact, some companies require that employees justify in writing at least once per year the productivity gains and benefits that they have achieved via telecommuting.

Senior management often sees significant cost savings in telecommuting. Instead of providing and paying for one office per employee many companies are now providing one guest office per two or three employees. Employees use the guest office only when they need to come in for meetings or other reasons. Thus, the company dramatically lowers its cost of office space. Some California communities are trying to cut down on commuting and air pollution by mandating that companies can only have three parking spaces for every five employees or even for every other employee.

Although not every middle manager is comfortable with the remote management of people, telecommuting appears to be a trend that is here to stay, and the extranet is likely to be the preferred tool of geographically challenged or remote managers.

Senior management also encourages remote access to lower the substantial cost of managing and upgrading the desktop. Various consultants and authors estimate this cost at $6,000–$8,000 annually per PC on a desktop. One way to lower this cost substantially is via remote access and automated software distribution. There are now products on the market from companies like Mirimba that periodically poll remote users and update their desktop automatically. There is a transmitter on a server that talks to a tuner with a unique fingerprint or identifier on the desktop. The conversation identifies what software on the desktop needs to be upgraded down to the byte level.

Thus, if only one byte of code needs to be updated on the desktop, one byte only will be sent from the server over the network to update the desktop. This implies that each user will operate a desktop that is unique and personalized and that is running a unique version of application code. There will now be thousands of versions of application code running at any given time. The file conflicts that often exist because users are attempting to run incompatible versions of code will be resolved by the tuners and transmitters. Repeaters on different nodes of the network may be required to move the software updates or tuner transmitter conversation across a large network.

Remote software distribution programs promise to make remote access to the latest application code of interest to the end user reality rather than exception. These programs will improve the odds that remote users can run the applications they want to when they want to when working from home or other remote location.

New software distribution technology is likely to dramatically enhance the number of new versions of software available to users and to dramatically decrease the time to distribute new versions of the software. For example, new versions of application software used to be developed and distributed to customers every 18 months or so. Now, a new version of software can be beta tested and distributed in a few hours or less. This raises the whole question of what is a new "version" of software. Is it a one byte change, a one line change, a one module change, or a change to every module of the program? From a user perspective any change in functionality probably feels like a new "version" of the software. Automated software distribution is likely to lead to greater control by information systems managers rather than less control. This is because information systems managers already have lost control of the desktop. Often, information systems management does not know what version of code is running where without doing an expensive manual inventory. At least with automated software distribution systems, information systems managers can ask a server to print out a list of what version of what software is running where. Even if it takes transmitters and tuners time to build the list, it will still be an advance over manual software inventories!

It is often the case that Internet, intranet, and extranet access proceeds through predictable stages as the enterprise becomes more comfortable with these technologies. Often Internet access for an enterprise begins with e-mail and proceeds to file transfer, telnet, or control of remote systems, and indexing of what is available on the intranet or extranet. Next comes web access for http and text documents.

The indexing is often a challenge because data are frequently stored on multiple inconsistent systems and there is no common methodology available to obtain the data. Usually, access and data retrieval policies implemented through standards and templates are needed to address this problem. There is frequently a need for indexers and crawlers or programs to find information on the intranet and extranet right away or within the first six months of operation because of the often explosive growth of intranet and extranet use. Many users want to index not just http files but all file types on the network including text, spread sheet, power point, and other file types. In effect, the users are looking for a data warehouse type of solution. If users can't quickly find the information that they want on the extranet or intranet, this can quickly threaten to wreck the entire extranet and or intranet project.

Fairly quickly the need for access to pictures and graphics is recognized. However, at least in a business, setting the pictures and images needed are directly tied to the business and are not necessarily the fancy graphics used to decorate many web pages. In fact the decorations can be a problem in the sense that the fancy graphics take time to download across the network and thereby can decrease overall network performance and user satisfaction. The need for streaming audio and video may be the last stage reached because of the widespread availability of substitutes for some applications of these technologies. Telephones and televisions are widely available and practical solutions for some audio and video needs like chat sessions.

The need for push and multicast technology is increasingly being recognized as intranets and extranets span enterprises. Although the desire of employees for the latest stock quotes or sports information may not increase their productivity, push technology can be used to deliver this information to employee desktops and thereby prevent employees from repeatedly connecting to and accessing the network to find this information. Thus, push technology can make the network more efficient and decrease the amount of time that employees spend repeatedly connecting to the same web servers to obtain updates to the topics that interest them. Push technology can be a useful tool for managing intranet and extranet access and for load balancing. Likewise, access requests can be redirected to web servers known as proxy servers that can service requests and provide information from a machine close to the requester.

Some enterprises have been known to encourage the creation and management of personal web sites. Although the business purpose of many of these web sites is not immediately obvious, they do give the individuals creating and maintaining them considerable training and practice in using web technologies and also help the staff get to know each other's interests and hobbies. Personal web sites also tend to increase the demand for extranet and intranet access as users access personal web sites to learn more about their colleagues and to share information on hobbies and personal interests.

Stating the business case for remote access is a critical piece of the extranet remote access challenge. It is an exercise that all of those working with extranets in commercial enterprises can expect to go through many, many times. Unfortunately, sometimes people become so fascinated with the technology that they overlook the business justification or just assume that everyone else is as excited about extranets, intranets, and Internet as they are. This is a mistake that is likely to eventually hurt extranet projects as well as personal careers even among technologists.

It is wise to think carefully about the business justification for every request for extranet, intranet, or Internet access and to have a simple but compelling business justification always on hand. "Simple or easy to understand and compelling" are the essence of a good business justification for many activities and projects not just extranet, intranet, and Internet projects. Some of the best business justifications for extranet access involve things like enhancing the ability to collaborate and communicate better and faster with suppliers, business partners, employees, and customers in different parts of the world and in different time zones.

Effective business justifications frequently cite specific examples of the ways in which extranet access can lead to personal productivity enhancements on specific projects. For example, a project manager in a pharmaceutical company might give examples of how access to an extranet shortened the time necessary to gain Food and Drug Administration approval for a new drug or decreased the amount of paperwork required thereby increasing productivity while lowering expenses.

Often extranet, intranet, and Internet access will justify themselves once these things get up and rolling. To pick an extreme example, just consider the increase in electronic transactions occurring at most leading financial houses these days. In their book, *The Judas Economy: The Triumph of Capital and the Betrayal of Work*, Wolman and Colamosca report that in the early 1970s the total amount of financial trades by American enterprises on American exchanges for an entire year amounted to less than the gross national product.

However, with the introduction of supercomputers and fast data networks by the mid-1990s the total trades of the financial sector of the United States economy per year were 30 to 40 times the gross national product of the United States economy. In fact it has been estimated that in 1995 the total trades of several United States financial firms each exceeded the total gross domestic product of the United States or about $6.5 trillion in 1995.

Computers and networks may not have caused this growth but they certainly made this volume of trading possible. If nothing else, these numbers present a strong business justification for planning for growth when it comes to designing and implementing intranet and extranet projects.

Of course, not every business justification for extranet, intranet, and Internet access is a good one. Described below are some examples of proposed justifications for access and extranet projects that were in fact shot down by management or those who have to pay for things and show an economic return from them.

One large multinational firm had a fully automated employee travel expense reimbursement system available on every desktop. However, the expense reimbursement system did not have a web front end and was pretty much character based and nongraphical. Management shot down a proposal to redesign the application by adding a web-based front end and fancy graphics. Although the new redesigned application might have been more fun to look at and available like many other applications over the web, it would not have generated enough incremental business benefit to the enterprise to justify the cost of redesigning and rewriting the application.

However, other enterprises have found enough business benefits in terms of the less steep learning curve for applications with a consistent web-based front end to justify similar projects. Thus, improving the appearance of and access to an application through design and implementation of a web-based front end may or may not meet the business justification requirements of different firms. Success often depends on the clarity and importance of the business case that accompanies the project proposal.

Sometimes, people generate proposals to make telephone and employee directories available via extranets and intranets. This can be a good idea if business partners and suppliers need this information and making it available to them will not create too many security risks. However, sometimes these projects are proposed because someone thinks that it would be neat to have a really graphical and colorful telephone and employee directory. If this is the true reason for the project, management is not likely to be impressed or excited about funding the project.

Proposals to make policies and procedures available over extranets and intranets often encounter similar difficulties. The right question to ask in developing such a proposal is what is the additional business benefit to the enterprise of implementing such a project.

After all, if in fact these policies and procedures are rarely referred to and used by employees or business partners then there would not seem to be much reason to spend money and resources to make them accessible over an extranet or intranet. If, on the other hand, the policies and procedures are frequently referred to and used then paper costs may be reduced and accessibility increased by making the policies and procedures accessible from an extranet or intranet. Again, worrying about business justification is not something that many technologists may enjoy doing, but it is absolutely required to give the project any reasonable chance of success.

Remote Dial Up and Extended LAN Access

One can connect the enterprise to the home or to the remote office with either a dial up telephone line or with a dedicated high speed line with a router or bridge with an ethernet connection on the end of it (see Note 4.1).

NOTE 4.1 ━━━━━━━━━━━▶

Remote Access Solutions   →   Dial up

→   Cable modem

The dial up approach is the best choice to implement when users travel or roam about from location to location. The cable modem approach is the best choice to implement when dealing with a remote office in a fixed location. Besides requiring special hardware and software in the form of a cable modem, this approach also requires an ISDN or other high-speed line to deliver maximum benefit.

Both the cable modem and the dial up approaches extend the enterprise local area network to remote locations. Cable modems and related software are beginning to offer some sophisticated management options for controlling the costs and ensuring the network security of telecommuting and working at home. For example, there are systems that automatically set up remote connections and tear down the remote connections at certain times of the day in order to save on telephone line costs.

In addition, there are systems that automatically call back or dial up certain locations at certain times of the day for both security and cost control purposes. For example when someone seeks access to the network claiming to be a sales rep calling from a remote office, the system hangs up and calls the remote office location back to ensure that the call is coming from an authorized location.

In addition, there are systems that periodically ping the equipment in the remote office and take down the connection if the remote equipment does not respond as expected. This is done to save money on connect charges. Push technologies can also be used to control or limit connection costs when employees are repeatedly dialing up the home office to check on things like the price of their shares of company stock. This activity is likely to be very common in a period of a stock run up or down. File caching products are also available to store files locally on remote clients or browsers and servers and thereby reduce transmission costs and delays. File caching software is required on both the server and client or browser side of the network in order to synchronize what gets cached.

Shell scripts are also available to run remote systems via remote software or command shell controls. Finger software enables network managers to identify who is using the network at any given time. Hot swapable back up remote access servers and power supplies are usually implemented to guarantee the reliability of the remote access system.

Both the cable modem and dial up remote access solutions require equipment policies and procedures to be effective. In other words, the enterprise that implements these solutions will need to decide who receives cable modems and who doesn't, who receives laptops and who doesn't, and what other equipment and software employees receive for working at home or remotely. Often, there will be disagreements between employee groups as to who should work remotely and who should not. These same types of policy questions and more come up with respect to business partners who want to work with the enterprise via an extranet. Often business partners want help acquiring remote access equipment and software in addition to business information from the enterprise.

There are enterprises that require employees and business partners to justify on an annual basis their need to work remotely and their need for the equipment and software that goes with the remote work. This continual business justification will probably fade somewhat as business managers become more comfortable with remote work and extranets. There are also filter technologies that can be used to prevent access by employees to socially undesirable Internet addresses.

One of the greatest challenges to the enterprise on implementing remote access schemes is providing help desk support to remote locations. This requires not only the training of the help desk support team in remote access and telecommunications technologies, but also the providing of a multiple telephone lines or channels to the remote location so that end users and the help desk support team can talk over another telephone line or channel while fixing a problem on a separate data line or channel. Help desk support personnel are no longer able to walk down the hallway to the end user's office. The end users now may be thousands of miles away from the physical location of the help desk support team.

The information technologies and tools used on the enterprise local area network today are very likely to be used in the home or in remote offices shortly. "As the local area network goes so goes the home," is a common saying at networking conferences and expositions today. This convergence is likely to grow stronger with time and will provide ever greater challenges for the help desk support team. To make this convergence practical and useful the wide area network will need to become as reliable and convenient to use as the local area network.

Enterprise Class Access Solutions with Multiple Channels per Port

Enterprise class solutions for extranet access usually include high-speed connection devices which allow multiple channels of connections per physical port. Each physical port may handle one or two dozen logical ports by managing bandwidth. Usually, this equipment is dedicated to channel management and removes the requirement for maintaining huge pools of modems to receive single calls and to set up single connections. Usually, a new connection and session is set up every time a user dials into the network with a modem. The constant creation and deletion of connections and sessions that occur with modem pools as users dial in and hang up creates heavy overhead on the network and often causes end users to perceive poor network or system performance.

Remote access concentrators, channel management software, and bandwidth management protocols now make it possible to have multiple channels per connection and to run multiple applications per session. For example, users can open a window to a remote system from their current session, enter shell commands, and close the window to the remote system. The remote system will process the user's shell commands while the user runs applications on the local system. The important point to understand about all this is that users can now run multiple tasks and retrieve data multiple times from the same remote system without shutting down and starting up connections and sessions each and every time. This dramatically lowers network and server overhead and improves the total system performance experienced by the end user.

Dedicated vs. Hybrid Systems

Remote access solutions come in two basic flavors; namely, dedicated and hybrid solutions.

The hybrid remote access solutions are often built on top of popular operating systems like an NT server. The great advantage of these systems is that they are inexpensive in that they come bundled with the operating system much as remote access server comes bundled with NT server. The disadvantage of hybrid systems is that they attempt to do more than one task at a time. This sometimes leads to performance or reliability issues if there are several thousands of users on the network.

The dedicated remote access solutions are often hardware devices. Their advantage is that they only do remote access and therefore are often higher performance and more reliable than are hybrid solutions. However, the dedicated solutions tend to be expensive. They are usually not bundled with anything else.

Increasingly hybrid systems are being offered that are optimized for remote access. These solutions combine relatively low cost with improved performance and reliability for remote network access.

Extranet Protocol Solutions

Extranet protocols are being defined and published at a dizzying rate. Ultimately, this is good news for consumers because this will result in a more competitive market and in products that interoperate well together. However, the acronyms can become overwhelming at times. To help you sort out the acronym soup, here is a list of some of the newer protocols and a brief description of what each of these protocols does.

Table 4.9 *Extranet Protocol Acronyms Explained*

L2FP—(Layer 2 Forwarding Protocol.) This protocol was originally introduced by Cisco Systems and negotiates the TCP/IP link level handshake and connections between each end of a tunnel.

PPTP—(Point to Point Tunneling Protocol.) This protocol also negotiates the TCP/IP link level handshake and connections between each end of a tunnel. It was original proposed by Microsoft. There is a discussion going on in standards bodies about combining L2FP and PPTP into one layer, 2 tunneling protocol called appropriately enough L2TP.

L2TP—(Layer 2 Tunneling Protocol.) See the definition and history of PPTP given above (see Note 4.2).

> **NOTE 4.2** ⟶
>
> TCP/IP Layer 2 Protocols → L2FP + PPTP = L2TP

PAP—(Password Authentication Protocol.) This is designed to define security procedures for authenticating user passwords.

CHAP—(Challenge Handshake Authentication Protocol.) This protocol defines the handshaking or communication necessary to authenticate users who can have access to the extranet (see Note 4.3).

Table 4.9 *Extranet Protocol Acronyms Explained (Continued)*

NOTE 4.3 ━━━━━━━━━━▶

Authentication Protocols   →   PAP

→   CHAP

MLP—(Multi-Link Protocol.) This is a bandwidth or channel management protocol.

MLP+—(Multi-Link Protocol +.) This is a more advanced version of the previous protocol.

BACP—(Bandwidth Allocation Control Protocol.) This protocol and its relatives allow network managers to allocate specific amounts of bandwidth to specific network tasks. For example, the network manager can assign 10% of the available bandwidth to moving e-mail and 20% of network bandwidth to web server access, and the rest of the network bandwidth to something else. The network manager can reserve network bandwidth or prevent end users from using a percentage of the network bandwidth at all. Use of this protocol should make contracting for specific level of service agreements for extranets more practical (see Note 4.4).

NOTE 4.4 ━━━━━━━━━━▶

Bandwidth of Channel Management Protocols   MLP

→   MLP +

→   BACP

IPSec—(This is a security protocol for the IP part of TCP/IP.) IP stands for Internetworking Protocol.

Many of these and other extranet access protocols are likely to be combined in the future.

Because of the diversity in technical environments likely to be encountered in implementing an extranet, open systems and platform independent browsers are an important part of the extranet access solution. The advantage of using open systems is that they increase the flexibility of solutions and make it easier to modify solutions in the future as environments and technologies change. Platform independent browsers help solve the access problem created by the diversity of the technical environments because they work in more than one technical environment and on more than one platform.

Extranet Access Security Paradigms

There are three basic security paradigms that apply to access of an extranet. I will define these extranet security paradigms here. There is more detailed information on extranet security in the chapter on security.

The oldest and most widely understood paradigm for controlling access to an extranet and to networks in general is based upon use of something that only a legitimate end user is expected to have namely a password or pass phrase. A newer paradigm for controlling access to an extranet is based on the use of something that only a legitimate end user can be expected to know like a birth date or hire date. The third paradigm for controlling access to an extranet is based upon personal identification of a legitimate end user via a personal identification number, retinal scan, or fingerprint.

Many extranet security schemes implement all three of these models. Of course, in some sense, the tighter the security the less convenient it is for end users to use the network. Thus, there is an ease of use versus security trade off decision to be made. Users especially like a single point of login for access to everything on the network. Users do no like to enter multiple passwords or personal identification numbers to gain access to their desktop, again for access to an extranet, and yet again for access to a remote sever. Multiple password protection is especially a problem for those people who use the network infrequently because they will have trouble remembering all of the passwords and personal identifiers that they will need to access a remote server. These users want one password and one authentication procedure to let them into anything on the network. They only want to go through a login authentication procedure once.

Synchronization of User Lists on Access Servers and Home Gateways

This is one of the harder problems of access for extranets because user lists on network access servers and home gateways tend to drift apart with the normal changes in staffing and in enterprise organization. Enterprise solutions provide synchronization engines and software to automatically synchronize these lists. In fact, larger networks including extranets tend to have their own name and Internetworking Protocol address servers at least partly to synchronize names and Internetworking Protocol addresses across the network.

Business Challenges and Risks of Extranets

The major business challenge and risks from extranets come from the fact that in allowing access to an extranet you are allowing some outsiders to have the same information normally available only to those inside the enterprise. Many businesses feel that the sharing of at least some internal information with business partners dramatically increases the amount of communication and collaboration between all members of the business team and thereby increases creativity.

Other businesses feel that sharing of too much information can be counterproductive. There have been cases of competitors going to public web sites to gain information that can be used to compete against the owner of the web site. Channel conflicts can result if, based upon information received from an extranet, distributors feel that they are not being treated fairly. If you let some of your distributors or employees have access to your extranet and not others you should expect to hear complaints from those who are not allowed access. Deciding when and how much information to share over an extranet is likely to be a new experience for many managers.

In fact, extranets often seem to go through the stages of growth described below. In the first stage, the extranet is used to extend or complement other forms of information and communication technology. Thus forms that were formerly faxed to business partners may be made available over the web. In the second phase, the extranet is used to exchange information that is personal to a business partner. Thus in the second stage delivery schedules for shipments to a particular business partner are made available to only that partner over an extranet. In the final stage, actual business transactions are conducted over an extranet including exchanges of credit card numbers or payments. The need for better security and the degree of business risk increases with each stage of growth.

Challenges and Solutions to Global Extranet Access

The challenges of implementing a global extranet include all of the challenges to implementing a domestic extranet and more. These additional challenges include personnel security, physical security of equipment and software, conflicting legal requirements of different countries, differing technical standards for the same technology in different countries, differing pricing levels for the same services in different countries, and monopolistic telecommunications markets in different countries.

In spite of these daunting challenges, solutions have begun to appear to the problem of implementing global extranets as well as access from anywhere on the planet to such extranets. These solutions include global 800 numbers, use of dial back procedures, use of GSM telephones, use of global positioning systems to manage data security and encryption, and outsourcing of global extranet infrastructure to companies like IBM, ATT, and BBN.

The problem of personnel security is one that companies seldom worry about in the United States and Canada, but can be a serious problem when installing or setting up networks overseas. For example, some companies see Eastern Europe and the former Soviet Union as hot opportunities for providing Internet services and network infrastructure services in general. Unfortunately, kidnapping and abduction is a common problem in this area and foreigners are frequently targets. Thus, the issue of personnel security is one that cannot be avoided if you are planning to build your own network infrastructure to support an extranet in some parts of the world.

The issue of physical security of computers, telecommunications equipment, and software is similar in many ways to personnel security. In many parts of the world, you cannot just assume that equipment will be safe from theft or physical attack. There are parts of Africa where armed guards will need to be hired to ensure that equipment does not disappear or does not get stolen only to be sold back to the original owners.

One of the more complex challenges to actual implementation of a global extranet arises from the complexity and inconsistency of different legal systems. For example, it is illegal for Swiss banks to release any information whatsoever about their customers including who they are. This is very different from the situation in the United States where banks commonly use lists of their largest corporate customers in advertising campaigns and as references. Such behavior by Swiss banks would be fraud in Switzerland.

This conflict of laws could become a major problem for a Swiss bank with a major branch in the United States connected by an extranet to the bank's home office in Switzerland. If the Swiss bank were required by a subpoena from a United States court to release the names of its customers it could be breaking the law in Switzerland. The bank can't win in this scenario. If it doesn't release the customer names then it violates United States law.

If it does release the customer names then it violates Swiss law. Moreover, some lawyers feel that any data that comes into the United States from a foreign country is subject to United States laws and to the laws of the country of origin. Thus, the Swiss bank probably wants to prevent certain kinds of data from crossing its extranet at all.

The conflict of laws problem is perhaps the most severe when it comes to the subject of security and encryption. The United States Munitions Act strictly limits the export of encryption technology and encryption devices. Moreover, in some countries, such as France, any encryption whatsoever by civilian companies or individuals is illegal and can subject violators to prosecution. Thus, even the encryption of your laptop files on your hard drive is illegal. Worse yet, certain high-performance laptops are actually classified as munitions under United States law and cannot be exported or taken out of the United States at all.

Pornography laws also create challenges to the development and implementations of extranets. America Online was recently prosecuted by Germany because some America Online users sought to move pornography over the Internet. In some countries, if the on-line provider exercises any editorial control whatsoever over content then it is required by law to prevent access to and movement of pornography over the network. If, on the other hand, the on-line provider exercises no editorial control whatsoever over content so that it is in effect a common carrier of data then it faces no such legal requirements.

These laws are often enforced on a selective basis and are used to punish politically unpopular companies. All of these laws are rapidly changing, and one should consult both local and international lawyers before building and implementing an extranet that spans multiple countries.

Differing technical standards in different parts of the world also create extranet access challenges. For example, in the United States standards for leased data lines include T1 and T3 standards for specific line speeds. T1 and T3 equivalents are not available in Europe.

Instead the Europeans offer E1 and E3 leased data line standards. E1 and E3 data rates do not correspond to T1 and T3 data rates. This means that if your extranet includes both sets of leased line standards then the network will operate at the lowest line speed standard in the network. This is not a show stopper but is something to be aware of as you design your global extranet.

There are substantial price differences for similar telecommunications services in different parts of the world. For example, it is five or six times cheaper to call Switzerland from California than it is to call California from Switzerland. Often, hotels add substantial surcharges to international and credit card calls. Some of the price differences result from the fact that deregulation of the telecommunications industry has proceeded far faster in the United States than in other parts of the world. Thus, in many parts of the world the local Post Telephone Telegraph (PTT) service is a government monopoly that does not want competition from extranets or any form of private network. Therefore, companies are required to send their data over the X.25 PTT network at relatively high prices. Although many countries are planning to deregulate their telecommunications industry in order to make it more competitive, much of the deregulation has yet to occur and it may be a crime not to use the facilities provided by the local PTT.

However, the good news is that solutions to the problems of global extranet access have recently appeared. One solution is to outsource your extranet network infrastructure to companies like Digital Equipment Corporation, IBM, ATT, or BBN. All of these companies move your data across international boundaries and will worry about dealing with local governments and PTTs. You will have to pay for the service but you'll sleep better at night.

Another solution is to use satellite connections to avoid the challenges of renting local leased data lines or to use call back procedures to achieve the lowest possible telephone rates. This works fine unless it violates the local laws that were written to protect the monopoly status of the local PTT.

GSM phones and global positioning systems are also solutions to the challenge of global extranet access. GSM telephones are special cellular telephones that can be used from anywhere in the world. They are often cheapest to use when used where they are bought.

Thus, a company might buy two GSM telephones to connect the United States and Europe and use each telephone in the region where it was purchased.

Global positioning sensors have been built into laptop computers so that the home office computer knows the location of the laptop trying to access it. The home office computer then adjusts the type of encryption used to be consistent with the laws of the location of the laptop or refuses to connect at all if the global position of the laptop is deemed to be too dangerous or unfavorable. The number and efficacy of solutions to the problem of accessing global extranets is exploding, and many countries are rushing to change their laws and customs in this area for fear of being shut out of emerging Internet and electronic markets.

Case Study

I end this chapter with a brief discussion of the Cisco Connection Online because I think that Cisco Systems has done a good job of solving many of the access problems and issues discussed in this chapter. I've mentioned Cisco before, but here I'd like to address some of the ways in which their web site and on-line operation has successfully addressed access issues related to extranets. According to the article "E-Commerce Bonanza: Is It Real or Imagined?" (Pang, March 1998), Cisco's electronic commerce web site is accessible by 45,000 customers around the globe, has 80,000 registered users, 3.5 million hits per day, and presently handles about 40% of Cisco's revenues.

Although Cisco Systems originally spent a lot of time and effort building its own tools, transaction programs, and application programming interfaces to develop and implement its extranet it now plans to buy off-the-shelf products whenever possible to maintain and improve its extranet. Cisco is now considering adding a third T3 line through Digital Island, a Hawaiian Internet Service Provider, to ensure high performance, availability, and accessibility to its extranet. In addition, Cisco Systems is evaluating a broad collection of off-the-shelf push, search, application framework, customer profiling, content generation, and electronic commerce products. According to the article, Cisco is considering replacing Apache servers with Netscape's Commerce Server. However, Cisco is also customizing the messaging application programming interfaces for large accounts.

What the Cisco example shows is that while substantial progress can be made toward solving accessibility problems with off-the-shelf products there remain situations in which large accounts and extranet partners with considerable business clout can demand and receive customized solutions. However, the need for customization should decline as standards for extranet access and operations become widespread.

Chapter Summary

The discussion in this chapter has explored the emerging solutions to the problems and challenges of extranet access. In some ways these challenges are growing because extranet access is growing, but the good news is that solutions are growing and multiplying as well. Cisco System's efforts to address extranet accessibility issues with off-the-shelf products like Netscape's Commerce Server, T3 lines, application framework technologies, and electronic commerce packages is a good example of this.

This whole area is one of explosive if not to say cataclysmic change. Some authors have argued that there has been nothing like the dramatic growth of the Internet, intranets, and extranets in the entire history of our planet. Although the claim seems overly dramatic to this writer, there is no question about the fact that the growth of these things is truly extraordinary. The growth of the Internet, intranets, and extranets can only be likened to the early spread of the telephone or of television throughout society.

This means that as one designs and implements access solutions, one must plan for rapid and profound change. This explains much of the emphasis and controversy within the high-tech industry on things like emerging standards, open systems, and modular design. Everyone is fearful of being locked into an older design or technology when things change and designing for change with open systems, standards, modular design, and adaptive systems is seen as a solution to the challenge of change.

However, growth and change have social as well as technology implications. This is especially true when it comes to the topic of web access and moving information across a network and international borders. There are societies and cultures within societies that believe that whomever manages or owns an intranet or extranet is fully responsible and liable for any and all information that gets served up over that network. Responsibility and liability is not just for the accuracy or truthfulness of the information provided but also for the social, moral, and ethical acceptability of the information provided. This can place enterprise owners of intranets and extranets and their managers in strange and risky positions. Thus, the least risky strategy for some extranet owners in certain countries may be to adopt the attitude and practices of common carriers of data and information in order to limit their liability for moving inaccurate or morally questionable content to that of a common carrier of information. In some countries this strategy will not work at all, and there is no way for the owner of an intranet or extranet to avoid legal liability for the quality, accuracy, and moral acceptability of information moved across the network.

The high velocity of business and technology change imply that owners of extranets and intranets can expect to face major disagreements between employees, business partners, and customers about who should and who should not be granted access to an extranet.

Is excluding some business partners and not others from extranet access or excluding some customers and not others from extranet access a form of discrimination that violates the law? Enterprises will need to develop new policies and procedures to deal with this question.

The high velocity of business and technology change also implies that owners of extranets and intranets can expect disagreements with governments over who should and who should not have access to extranets and intranets. Thus, some governments have decreed all data encryption by civilian personnel or companies to be felonies. Other governments place export restrictions on encryption equipment and software or even on moving encrypted data across their borders. Many of these laws are changing, and the United States government is considering an exception to its restrictions on the export of encryption equipment and software to allow the export or use of encryption equipment and software at least as powerful as that sold locally. However, this change is not yet law.

The best way to deal with constant change is to be constantly learning. This means that you should get involved with the technical, business, and social organizations at the forefront of intranet and extranet technology. Networld + Interop, the Internet Association, and numerous business organizations are all very active in this area. There are numerous industry conferences where excellent information on the challenges to and solutions for extranet access are discussed. Some of the better ones are the conferences and expositions sponsored by DCI Conferences and Expositions of Andover, Massachusetts and the conferences and expositions sponsored by Software Productivity Group of Marlboro, Massachusetts in addition to the spring and fall Networld + Interop conferences in Atlanta, Georgia and Las Vegas, Nevada.

In summary, this chapter has covered:

▶ The explosion occurring in Internet and extranet access.

▶ The reasons why people want remote access to the enterprise via an extranet and how they justify their need to management.

▶ The two primary types of remote access to the extranet. 1. Remote dial-up access. 2. Extending the LAN to the small office home office via routers and bridges with Ethernet connections.

▶ Enterprise class solutions with multiple channels or connections per port.

▶ Management of access options in terms of automated ping, automated dial up, and automated build up and tear down of connections.

▶ Hybrid vs. dedicated hardware and software systems for remote access.

▶ Tunneling, bandwidth control, and security protocols such as L2FP, L2TP, PPTP, PAP, CHAP, MLP, MLP+, BACP, and IPSec.

▶ Different security paradigms such as what the user knows, what the user has, and unique user identifier systems for controlling and managing remote access.

▶ Synchronization of user lists on network access servers and home gateways.

▶ The business benefits and risks of remote access to the enterprise via the extranet,

▶ The challenges and solutions to remote access presented by going international or global including issues of personnel security, physical security of hardware and software, encryption/decryption laws, differing legal systems, and competitive environments.

▶ A case study.

In a future chapter, we will discuss extranet security. This topic is very closely related to the topic of extranet access so you might want to read the chapter on security next although you don't have to in order to understand the rest of the text.

5

Highly Available and Reliable Extranets

Chapter Objectives

This chapter describes solutions for highly available and reliable extranets. Availability and reliability are key success factors for extranets because by definition extranets are highly visible to business partners, customers, others outside the organization. In some sense the availability and reliability of an extranet puts the credibility of the entire organization on the line because of the extreme visibility of an extranet.

This chapter discusses:

▶ A brief history of web site implementations.

▶ Who should be involved in the design and implementation of highly available and reliable extranet web sites and how long should the design and implementation process take.

▶ Setting expectations for highly available and reliable extranets.

▶ Benchmarks and measurable performance and reliability goals for highly available and reliable extranets.

▶ Round robin domain name server address resolution techniques as a way of building highly available and reliable extranet web sites.

▶ What happens to round robin domain name server address resolution when a server goes down for any reason.

▶ Round robin domain name server address resolution recovery techniques for downed servers.

▶ Intelligent querying of servers by clients and other servers through CORBA and DCOM, etc.

▶ The colocation solution to the challenge of building highly available and reliable extranet web sites.

▶ Wide area networking peer connection issues and solutions for building and implementing highly available and reliable extranets.

▶ Final recommendations for building and implementing highly available and reliable extranets.

▶ Examples of highly available and reliable extranets from industry.

▶ Product solutions for highly available and reliable extranets.

Web site technology has been evolving extremely rapidly. Along with this evolution has come more highly available and reliable web sites, intranets, and extranets. Progress with regard to new product offerings that support highly available and reliable extranets has been particularly encouraging and will be discussed at the end of this chapter. To put all of this in perspective it helps to look at the history of web site implementations.

A Brief History of Web Site Implementations

Not very long ago the typical web site design and implementation included use of Common Gateway Interface (CGI) scripting, Hypertext Markup Language (HTML), and of Hypertext Transport Protocol (HTTP), as shown in the top half of Figure 5.1.

Probably the weakest link in this chain of technology from the standpoint of web server availability and reliability was the fact that every time a browser on a desktop client queried a web site, a new connection and session was established from the desktop to the web server. When the session ended, the connection between web server and browser was broken down. This constant connection and disconnection of desktop to web server was a high overhead process that absorbed bandwidth on both networks and servers.

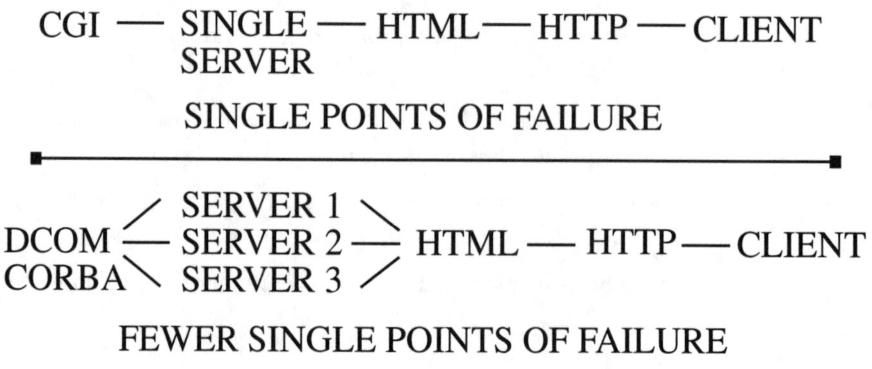

Figure 5.1
History of
Web Sites

CGI — SINGLE — HTML— HTTP — CLIENT
SERVER

SINGLE POINTS OF FAILURE

```
                  ╱ SERVER 1 ╲
     DCOM  ──  SERVER 2  ──→  HTML — HTTP — CLIENT
     CORBA ╲  SERVER 3  ╱
```

FEWER SINGLE POINTS OF FAILURE

Moreover, this process was not intelligent. In early web site implementations server status and availability was not monitored. Thus, if a web server was down or unavailable for any reason the browser on the desktop had no way of knowing this and would keep trying to make a connection even if the web server was not there. The early web server implementations also made no attempt to do load balancing between multiple web servers.

The early web site implementations can be described as centralized rather than distributed implementations because all of the different data types were placed on the same web server instead of on separate web servers. This not only leads to a single point of failure, namely the web server, being built into the implementation but also made analysis of availability and reliability problems difficult because either the entire system worked or didn't. It was difficult to break down availability and reliability problems into smaller pieces for purposes of analysis, repair, and test.

The bottom half of Figure 5.1 shows a more modern web site or extranet implementation. There is now more than one server in the implementation and different data types are placed on different servers. Thus, text might come to the desktop from one server, graphics from a second server, audio from a third server, and video from a fourth server.

In addition, the multiple web servers are continuously monitored as to their availability to process requests for information.

In the more modern web site implementation, there is no longer a single point of failure because of the redundancy that comes from distributing data across many servers. In addition, the segregation of different data types to different servers makes analysis of problems by breaking problems into smaller pieces easier. Moreover, the segregation of different data types to different servers means that even if one or two servers should go down or drop off the extranet for any reason at least some extranet functionality will remain and some data types will still be available over the extranet.

The bottom of Figure 5.1 also shows Distributed Component Object Method from Microsoft or DCOM and Common Object Request Broker Architecture or CORBA from Microsoft competitors. These are two standards by which clients or servers can communicate with or request various objects. The primary purpose of these standards is to promote code reusability and thereby enhance software development productivity.

However, use of these standards also improves communication between processes and enables parallel communications between desktops and clients. This means that every time a browser or desktop queries a web server a new connection and session does not have to be set up and torn down. This greatly improves the reliability and availability of an extranet.

The more modern web site implementation can be described as a distributed architecture or implementation in which objects communicate with and request each other via industry standard protocols. This minimizes single points of failure and the overhead from setting up and tearing down connections, allows problems to be analyzed and subdivided, and thereby improves the overall availability and reliability of the extranet.

Who Should Be Involved in the Design and Implementation of Extranets?

Some authors estimate that as many as 75% of the failures of extranet projects can be attributed to the failure of business and technical people to engage and communicate (see Note 5.1). In fact, many extranet projects begin with dramatically different views by technical and business people as to what an extranet is and the organizations goal in designing and implementing one. Many web sites start out as marketing sites designed to "get the word out" or to spread marketing and sales messages and evolve into sites for processing orders and other types of commercial transactions.

NOTE 5.1 ———————▶

Who's Involved and How Long Does It Take?

Business   One to twelve months

Technical

Design

The entire extranet project is at risk of failure if part of the organization building an extranet believes it to be a marketing site and another part of the organization believes it to be a site for processing commercial transactions. The part of the organization that wants a marketing extranet web site will not understand why the project cannot be completed in one to two months, and the part of the organization that wants a transaction processing extranet web site will not be satisfied with an extranet web site that skimps on security and transaction monitoring capabilities.

Clearly both technical and business people need to be an ongoing part of the extranet team. The word "ongoing" is used intentionally because much will change during the life of an extranet development and deployment project and these changes will need to be communicated and supported. For example, there will probably need to be both a Web Master to sort out the technical issues surrounding extranet web sites as well as content providers from the business side of things to deliver and keep current the information published over the extranet. A third member of the extranet development and implementation team needs to be an extranet designer. This is because Web Masters and content providers will be far too busy to worry about the full set of consequences that result from implementing this or that extranet architecture. The most effective extranet projects involve both end users and business partners in the design and implementation of the project because this helps set accurate expectations as to the goal and nature of an extranet.

As for resolving how long an extranet project should take, this author keeps hearing estimates of two months to one year to design and implement extranet web sites. The longer time period usually results from discovering and having to resolve telecommunications and technical infrastructure issues during the lifetime of an extranet project.

Setting Expectations for Availability and Reliability with Benchmarks and Statistics

Even after the entire organization has clear and consistent expectations for an extranet, the job of setting expectations for extranet availability, reliability, and performance is not over. The accumulation and study of usage and performance statistics can help a great deal here. Thus playback, interpretive, and inspection benchmark tests can all be used to set end user and management expectations of an extranet.

Inspection benchmark testing has gotten a bad name in the industry because inspection tests often fail to accurately predict how systems will behave when loaded with applications. Inspection tests frequently fire thousands of arbitrary transactions at the system undergoing test. However, those arbitrary transactions fail to accurately reflect the actual mix of transactions actually generated by applications. Whetstone testing is frequently cited as an example of an inspection test.

Interpretive bench mark tests try to mimic the behavior of actual applications and thereby give an accurate picture of system performance and degradation when loaded with actual applications. This can be a useful exercise when it is done right. Use of test scripts which drive Microsoft desktop applications to load up a system would be one example of interpretive benchmark testing.

The best form of benchmark testing from the standpoint of showing what system performance might be under actual use is playback testing. In playback testing, end user keystrokes are recorded and played back to a system undergoing test in order to load the system. Playback testing when done right gives the most accurate picture of what system performance under actual use might be (see Note 5.2).

NOTE 5.2 ────────▶

Types of Benchmarks

✓ Playback

✓ Synthetic

✓ Inspection

Identical test beds are needed

The phrase "testing done right" refers to the fact that benchmark testing is not easy and the performance of machines and systems can only be compared if the configurations are exactly the same and if the machines are powered up and down for each test.

In fact, much testing is done not so much to compare systems as to determine exactly when a given system begins to fail because it does not have enough RAM memory or other critical resource. Thus test data can help you determine exactly how much memory or other resource you need to ensure that your extranet is highly available and reliable.

Some extranet designers are aggressive in setting performance parameters for their extranet web sites. Latency is the delay between the time when an end user clicks on a web site or page icon and the page begins to appear on the end user's desktop. Throughput is the delay between the time the browser or desktop system starts to paint a page and finishes painting a page. Design goals of less than 5 seconds for latency and 5–10 seconds for throughput are considered aggressive but doable within industry (see Note 5.3).

NOTE 5.3 ────────▶

Latency and Throughput Goals

Latency < 5 sec

Throughput = 5–10 sec

Setting clear expectations for latency and throughput is important because no one will consider an extranet to be highly available and reliable if they have to wait a long time for a page of information to start appearing or to finish appearing on their desktop.

Round Robin Domain Name Server Techniques

Note 5.4 illustrates a round robin domain name server address resolution technique that is frequently used to do load balancing between Internet, intranet, and extranet web site servers. Although browsers request information from a server with one name, the domain name server redirects each request to any one of several servers with the same name but different TCP/IP addresses and thereby balances the load across several servers. This makes the whole system perform better and builds redundancy into an extranet.

NOTE 5.4 ——————————▶

Round Robin Name Resolution

Server 1   →   Requests 1, 5, 9

Server 2   →   Requests 2, 6, 10

Server 3   →   Requests 3, 7, 11

Server 4   →   Requests 4, 8, 12

Even if one server should fail entirely or be taken off-line for any reason, the other servers would continue to function and to answer requests from browsers for information. In fact, an extranet implementing round robin domain name server address resolution technique can recover from server down by simply redirecting requests to that server to a different server with the same name but a different TCP/IP address (see Notes 5.5 and 5.6).

NOTE 5.5 ——————————▶

Round Robin Name Resolution—Server Down

Server 1   →   Requests 1, 5, 9

Server 2   Requests 2, 6, 10

Server 3   →   Requests 3, 7, 11

Server 4   →   Requests 4, 8, 12

NOTE 5.6 ————————▶

Round Robin Name Resolution—Recovery

Server 1   →   Requests 1, 4, 7, 10

Server 2   Requests

Server 3   →   Requests 2, 5, 8, 11

Server 4   →   Requests 3, 6, 9, 12

An extranet implementing this type of round robin technique can be made even more highly available and reliable through continuous monitoring of the availability of web site servers to answer requests for information. If a server disappears or is unavailable for any reason, the domain name server simply redirects the request to another server that is up and available to answer requests.

In fact, intelligence can be built into the devices making requests for objects through DCOM and CORBA so that the requests go only to web site servers that are up and running (see Note 5.7).

NOTE 5.7 ————————▶

Intelligent Server Allocation

Server 1 busy   →   Client request redirected

Server 2 busy   →   Client request redirected

Server 3 ready   →   DCOM CORBA   →   Client request answered

Colocation or External Hosting Solution to Building

According to figures cited at the Windows NT/Intranet Conference in August of 1997 in San Francisco, the colocation or external hosting of web sites will be a two billion dollar business by the year 2000. Without a doubt, many Internet Service Providers are moving in the direction of offering their clients more than just Internet access. They are now offering servers in glass rooms and protected, secure areas on which their clients can place content for delivery over the Internet. In other words, clients can place their content on host machines external to their organization or "colocate" extranet content (see Note 5.8).

NOTE 5.8 ——————————▶

Colocation

Someone else provides servers and bandwidth
You provide content or other third parties do

Many organizations prefer the external hosting or colocation approach because it frees them from having to implement expensive network upgrades and other infrastructure projects. Instead, an organization can focus on delivering great content to its external hosting provider and let the provider worry about resolving infrastructure and network bandwidth issues.

However, colocation does not free an organization from having to develop and deliver high-quality web site content. Moreover, many colocation providers are experiencing an explosion of business and will not guarantee a maximum response time when a customer's server goes down or experiences availability and reliability problems.

Wide Area Connection Challenges and Solutions

The major wide area challenge for designing and implementing extranets is to get some kind of level of service agreement from your wide area Internet Service Provider (see Note 5.9). This is a challenge unless you are dealing with one of the very largest Internet Service Providers whose networks span the globe. This is because for the smaller Internet Service Providers their networks connect at peer points and packets of information have to cross multiple networks from different providers to reach their final destination. Thus, the smaller Internet Service Providers are reluctant to guarantee preset levels of service.

NOTE 5.9 ——————————▶

Robust and Reliable Extranets

✓ Same ISP on each end

✓ Watch for peer connects

✓ Visit ISP weather site

You should look for level of service agreements and consider going with a larger Internet Service Provider and paying higher rates to get the level of service guarantee that you need for your extranet. Thus, you should look for agreements in which a service which guarantees to get most of the packets there sometime is less expensive than a service which guarantees to get all of the packets there soon! You can also check out Internet Service Providers by going to the Internet weather site which regularly pings or tests different Internet Service Providers and reports their level of traffic congestion and performance.

Final Recommendations for Designing and Implementing

Here is s a list of specific recommendations for designing and implementing highly available and reliable extranets. Other approaches will work as well, but you may want to at least consider the following approach and modify it as appropriate for your business and technical environment.

▶ Use more than one web site server to increase the availability and reliability of your extranet.

▶ Consider Round Robin Domain Name Server Address Resolution as a way of load balancing across several extranet web servers.

▶ Separate different data types to different servers to guarantee at least partial functionality if a single web site server should fail.

▶ Continuously monitor servers and build intelligence into requests for objects via DCOM, CORBA, or other industry standards.

▶ Go with a fast but proven network backbone technology like FDDI, etc.

▶ Make sure that business and technical people as well as a designer are fully engaged and an ongoing part of your extranet team.

▶ Set accurate expectations for your extranet via accumulation of and publication of performance and usage statistics as well as project management discipline.

▶ Seek level of service agreements from your Internet Service Providers.

▶ Consider external hosting or colocation if you wish to avoid some upgrade and infrastructure expenses.

Example of an Available and Reliable Extranet from Industry

One of the largest software companies in the world receives 30–40 million hits per day on its extranet web site servers (see Note 5.10). It uses round robin domain name server address resolution to spread this load across about seven servers and continuously monitors its servers as to their availability and performance statistics. In addition, this company places different data types on different servers and requires that business and technology personnel work as an ongoing team to deliver high-quality content to the web site servers and to keep the web site servers highly available and reliable. It has not colocated or externally hosted its content at least partly because it wants to build extranet expertise within its own company and staff. This company uses both its own and third-party products in its extranet.

NOTE 5.10 ⎯⎯⎯⎯⎯⎯⎯➤

A Reliable, Robust Extranet

7 servers + round robin DNS + 11 people = 30–40 million hits per day

---

Most extranets will not be as big as the one mentioned in this example. Some experts consider any extranet involving about 100 HTML pages or more and an audience of about 100 end users or more to be "an industrial strength web site" that requires load balancing, redundancy, security, high performance, and a high degree of availability and reliability. Many extranets will meet these criteria and need to be viewed as "industrial strength" and "mission critical" by their designers, implementers, and end users.

Amazon.com is another outstanding example of a highly reliable and available extranet web site. Amazon.com is an on-line bookstore that offers to sell two and one half million different books to consumers from anywhere in the world at any time night or day 365 days per year. Some of Amazon's primary concerns in designing an extranet were to design a system that would grow as Amazon's on-line business grows and would keep its business open and available around the clock. Amazon did this with high-performance UNIX web servers. The Hungarian Copyright Office managed to design and deploy an extranet to manage the collection and distribution of royalties and used it to triple its output without adding staff.

Product Solutions

There are now several load balancing product solutions on the market that not only implement round robin domain name server address resolution but that also sense which servers are up and available and direct queries only to servers that are actually available. These products and the results of testing them are described in detail in "A Well-Balanced Web" (Taschek, March 1998). The products range in price from $5,250 for a Fox Box Network Access Gateway to $39,990 for a Big/IP Server Array Controller Solution. Each of the products supports different Internet-related protocols like TCP, UDP, SMTP, HTTP, and SHTTP and has different fail over and fail safe characteristics.

The product characteristics that determine pricing are the numbers of ports and protocols supported, the ability to balance servers that reside in different geographies, the ability to sense the closest available server to the client requesting service by monitoring server response time over the network, fail over and fail safe characteristics, and the performance throughput of the product. Products vary in performance capabilities from those that can handle T1 line speeds to those that can handle T3 line speeds. The article cited above has a nice product table or matrix that summarizes this information.

The good news for the consumer and designer of extranets is that off-the-shelf product solutions are now available for highly available and reliable extranets. These solutions not only balance traffic effectively but also avoid continually sending requests to a downed server.

Chapter Summary

This chapter has taken a detailed look at extranet availability and reliability and offered specific recommendations for building and examples of highly available and reliable extranets (see Note 5.11). Although business and technical environments differ, you should at least consider the ideas discussed in this chapter and modify them as appropriate for your organization.

NOTE 5.11 ————————▶

Reliable and Robust Extranet Summary

✓ Analyze

✓ Design

✓ Test

✓ Implement

Specifically, this chapter has looked at:

▶ A brief history of web site implementations.

▶ Who should be involved in the design and implementation of highly available and reliable extranet web sites and how long should the design and implementation process take.

▶ Setting expectations for highly available and reliable extranets.

▶ Benchmarks and measurable performance and reliability goals for highly available and reliable extranets.

▶ Round robin domain name server address resolution techniques as a way of building highly available and reliable extranet web sites.

▶ What happens to round robin domain name server address resolution when a server goes down for any reason.

▶ Round robin domain name server address resolution recovery techniques for downed servers.

▶ Intelligent querying of servers by clients and other servers through CORBA and DCOM, etc.

▶ The colocation solution to the challenge of building highly available and reliable extranet web sites.

▶ Wide area networking peer connection issues and solutions for building and implementing highly available and reliable extranets.

▶ Final recommendations for building and implementing highly available and reliable extranets.

▶ Examples of highly available and reliable extranets from industry.

▶ Product solutions for highly available and reliable extranets.

Although the technology of highly available and reliable extranets has and will continue to advance rapidly, the organizational behavior challenges of designing and implementing highly available and reliable extranets still accounts for about 75% of the extranet projects that fail. Thus, considerable emphasis should be placed on project management and fully engaging both technical and business audiences when designing and implementing extranets.

6

Extranet Security

Chapter Objectives

The objective of this chapter is to discuss the major security challenges and problems of extranets and possible solutions to these security problems. Security is a function of policy and management as well as of technology; thus, this chapter more than any other in this book is a combined management and technology discussion.

Specifically, this chapter explores:

▶ Increasingly widespread social concerns with the confidentiality, integrity, and availability of information.

▶ The meaning of the words "extranet security."

▶ Examples of extranet information security policy guidelines and of extranet information security actions in light of the security, management, and administration challenges of personal web sites.

▶ Authentication with passwords or pass phrases, token cards, and biometric devices.

▶ Cryptographic solutions to the extranet security challenge.

▶ Firewall solutions to the extranet security challenge.

▶ Architectural and tunneling tradeoffs required to overcome the extranet security challenge.

▶ Some ethical and product solutions to the extranet security challenge.

▶ Example of a product solution.

▶ A summary of solutions for extranet security.

As you can probably guess from reading this list of chapter objectives, solving the extranet security puzzle requires a mixture of social, managerial, policy, and technology actions. I should point out up front that I believe that many of the security and privacy problems presented by extranets have been solved. Strong encryption and authentication techniques can be used to make extranets very secure indeed. It is in fact possible to track customers and gather marketing data over an extranet without enraging and offending all of your business partners, customers, and extranet end users. At the end of this chapter, I'll discuss some of the exciting new security practices and products that make this possible. Let's begin by looking at the current state of security and privacy concerns that pervade the United States and greatly influence the reaction of the public to the Internet, intranets, and extranets.

Public Concerns with Confidentiality, Integrity, and Availability

To say that the American public is greatly concerned with privacy, confidentiality, accuracy, and availability of information is a massive understatement.

For example, Ann Reilly Dowd summarizes the current state of this concern in an article entitled "How to Protect Your Privacy" (August 1997). She reports on a *Money Magazine* telephone poll of 550 Americans that showed that about 75% of those surveyed were very concerned with threats to their privacy, 67% were now more worried about threats to their privacy than they were five years ago, 80% of the women surveyed were worried about threats to their privacy, and 65% of the men surveyed were worried about threats to their privacy.

Moreover, concerns about privacy or confidentiality of data were clearly focused on specific areas. Thus, 88% of those surveyed were concerned with loss of social security numbers and personal identifiers, 83% of those surveyed were concerned with disclosure of financial records, and 70% were concerned with disclosure of medical information. About two thirds of those surveyed were concerned with eavesdropping on cellular telephone calls, sales and rental of personalized marketing lists, and employer surveillance.

Some of the greatest fears found by the survey were directly tied to the Internet and things like the Internet. Thus, 69% of those surveyed were worried about Internet companies collecting information on their family's buying preferences, and 64% of those surveyed were worried about Internet companies tracking their visits to world wide web sites. This was about the same percentage as were worried about the sale or rental of personalized marketing lists. Fewer respondents (55% of those surveyed) but not a lot fewer were worried about stores collecting and sharing information on their personal shopping habits.

The Meaning of the Words "Extranet Security"

As you can see from the above discussion there is great concern with keeping personal, financial, and medical information confidential. Likewise, there is great concern with protecting the integrity and accuracy of personal, financial, and medical information as well as with making the right information available to the right people at the right time. Thus, "extranet security" refers to protecting the confidentiality, integrity, and availability of the information traveling across or stored on the extranet at any given time.

Information Use and Confidentiality Policies

I hope the above discussion has convinced you of the fact that you need not only technology but also policies and practices to make your extranet secure.

Here are some examples of information security policies in the form of tables that you might want to expand upon and modify in order to increase the security of your extranet.

Table 6.1 *A Set of Extranet Information Security Policy Guidelines*

	Kind of Information	Source of Information	Destination of Information	Use of Information
1.	Price Lists	Marketing	Sales Reps Channels Partners Value Added Resellers etc.	To develop bids and proposals
2.	Product/Service Descriptions	Development	Sales Reps Channels Partners Value Added Reseller Marketing Customers etc.	To develop bids and proposals, to compare alternative solutions
3.	Competitive Information	Marketing/Sales	Sales Reps	To best the competition
4.	Testimonials/Customer References	Marketing	Sales Reps Prospects Channels Partners Value Added Resellers Customers etc.	To increase the bid/win ratio, to shorten the sales cycle

Table 6.1 *A Set of Extranet Information Security Policy Guidelines (Continued)*

	Kind of Information	Source of Information	Destination of Information	Use of Information
5.	Case Studies	Marketing	Sales Reps Prospects Channels Partners Value Added Resellers Customers etc.	To increase the bid/win ratio, to shorten the sales cycle
6.	Bug Fixes	Software Engineering	Field Service Engineers Customers	To increase customer satisfaction
7.	Engineering Designs	Engineering	Engineering Development Teams and Partners	To decrease time to market through collaboration and communication
8.	Project Schedules	Project Management	Project Team Members Project Stakeholders	To decrease project time and increase customer satisfaction through collaboration and communication
9.	Lists of Product Requirements	Product Management Engineering Marketing	Product Management Engineering Marketing	To decrease project time and increase customer satisfaction through collaboration and communication
10.	Readiness Review Documents	Project Management Cross Functional Project Team	Project Management Cross Functional Project Team	To increase customer satisfaction through collaboration and communication
11.	Announcements of special sales programs and incentives	Marketing and sales management	Sales Reps Channels Partners Value Added Resellers Prospects	To shorten the sales cycle, to gain market share etc.

Both Tables 6.1 and 6.2 are presented not as final or complete answers but only to start the reader thinking about what a set of extranet information security policy guidelines and a set of extranet information security actions should look like in his or her organization. Often, extranet information security policy guidelines and actions are a good deal longer and more detailed than those presented here.

Table 6.2 *A Set of Extranet Information Security Policy Actions*

	Kind of Information	Confidentiality of Information	Integrity of Information	Availability of Information
1.	Price List	Open or unencrypted during transmission and storage; pass phrase protected access control	Updated daily	24 hours/day 7 days per week or 24 × 7
2.	Discounts and Allowances List	Encrypted during transmission only; pass phrase protected access control	Updated twice per day	24 × 7
3.	Sales Reps Commissions	Encrypted during transmission and again for storage; pass phrase protected access control	Updated monthly	24 × 7

There are no final or black and white answers in the world of information security instead there are only trade offs to be made. Nothing illustrates this principle so well as the security, management, and administration issues surrounding the explosive growth of personal web sites across the enterprise. Ever since Microsoft made personal web server software available for any desktop running Windows 95 and other vendors made software available to run printers and other devices from any web page, individuals have rushed to create web sites on their desktop and even their laptop machines. As you can imagine, this has generated an explosion of security, management, and administrative concerns for the enterprise. Table 6.3 summarizes the personal web site debate.

As you can see from Table 6.3, the rapid growth of personal web sites has created enormous new opportunities and challenges for the enterprise. Some companies like Netscape have responded by giving every employee access to a server where they can publish their own web pages. Other companies have asked those developing their own personal web sites on their desktop or laptop machines to use standard operating systems and protocol software.

Still other companies urge employees developing personal web sites to look to certain servers for configuration information and software. Moreover, the growth of personal web sites is beginning to influence the growth of extranets because developers of personal web sites often want to share

Table 6.3 *Personal Web Site Pros and Cons*

Pros	Cons
1. Provides web technology training and experience to employees	1. Employees with personal web sites must do their own system management, administration, and security
2. Allows employees to easily share information and collaborate with colleagues	2. Information becomes hard to find
3. Allows employees to easily reach their own information from any desktop with a browser	3. If the desktop goes down the web site goes down
4. Allows employees to extend their desktops with agents and web server technology	4. Makes employees responsible for content generation and technology
	5. Removes web sites from Information Systems Management and Web Master control

information with all of their colleagues not just employees but business partners and nonemployees as well.

Authentication Practices and Procedures

The word "authentication" refers to the process of proving the identity of someone or something. This is a crucial part of securing an extranet because without it there can be no access control to the information and services available over an extranet. Many people are used to being "authenticated" or to having their identity proven when they attempt to cash a check at a bank and have to present a photo ID to the bank teller in order to prove that they are who they say they are or when they have to enter a personal identification number in order to prove that they are who they say they are when conducting a financial transaction over a touch tone telephone.

There are three categories of authentication and three types of authentication techniques that apply to the Internet, intranets, and extranets. All of these will be discussed in this chapter.

Anyone who has used a time share system has encountered user to host authentication in which users must prove their identity to a host computer in order to access the information and resources available on the host machine. Similarly, one host must authenticate or prove its identity to another host in order to access the information and resources available on another host machine. User to user authentication in which one user must prove his or her identity to another user in order to access the information and resources of the other user plays a large part in desktop to desktop tunneling and extranet communications.

The three types of authentication techniques most commonly encountered with the Internet, intranets, and extranets are the something you know technique, the something you have technique, and the something you are technique. Sometimes, one or two or all three of these techniques are used together to strengthen authentication and security.

The something you know or password and pass phrase technique is the technique that users most commonly encounter when interacting with computers and computer networks. The something you know technique is also the authentication procedure most commonly used by the Internet, intranets, and extranets. The effectiveness of this technique depends upon keeping the something you know secret. Thus, this technique is only as good as people and machines are at keeping secrets.

The something you have technique depends upon the possession of some kind of object and thus is only as secure as is possession of that object. If the object is lost, stolen, or loaned security is thereby compromised. Use of door and car keys are good examples of the something you have technique of security. Although the something you have technique is considered to be a weak security technique, it can be made much stronger by combining it with the something you know technique. For example, many banks and financial institutions require that their customers use both the something you know and something you have security techniques. These institutions require that their customers know a personal identification number and possess a plastic card in order to conduct financial transactions at their automated teller machines.

The something you are security technique is a fairly strong security technique that depends upon measuring some unique individual characteristic to prove identity. Examples of some of the characteristics typically measured are fingerprints, voices, retinas, and handwriting. The security assumption is that these are unique individual characteristics that are impossible or nearly impossible for the bad guys to duplicate. Unfortunately, these types of biometric measurements suffer from a number of drawbacks. Biometric devices are often expensive and operate within a range of values or tolerance. Tolerance is required because human characteristics are not perfectly constant but instead vary a bit from moment to moment and day to day. The need for tolerance means that occasionally biometric devices will make mistakes and confuse legitimate users with impostors. In addition, some users object to physical contact with heavily used biometric devices due to fear of infection and spread of disease.

In terms of extranets, the most popular types of authentication procedures are the something you know and the something you have procedures. Biometric devices are not in widespread use for all of the reasons given in the above paragraph. Authentication and access to most extranets today is controlled by passwords and pass phrases occasionally combined with some type of personal identity number that the user has. Most extranet users will encounter the something you know authentication procedure for user to host authentication in the form of static passwords, passwords used only once or one-time passwords, or trusted third-party procedures.

Static passwords authentication techniques are widely used on the Internet, intranets, and extranets. In these techniques, users are assigned account names along with a secret word or phrase known only to the user. Presentation of the correct account name and password or pass phrase will prove identity to a host machine. Static passwords and pass phrases can be changed by the users or host machine administrators. Although passwords and pass phrases are often sent across the wires from the users to the host machine and are thereby subject to theft by network eavesdroppers, passwords and pass phrases are usually stored on the host machine in a hashed file. Hashing both compresses and encrypts the stored passwords so that they are no longer in human readable form. When the user enters and sends his or her password or pass phrase to the host machine during login, the host machine hashes the password and compares the result to the passwords and pass phrases stored in the hash file. If there is a match with the information in the hash file, authentication occurs.

Of course this form of security works well only if users don't share or lose their passwords and pass phrases and if users pick unguessable passwords and pass phrases in the first place. Unfortunately, many studies have shown that end users don't behave as desired for purposes of ensuring host or network security. Thus, end users routinely disclose their passwords and pass phrases to coworkers and others, use the names of spouses and pets as passwords and pass phrases, choose standard dictionary words for their passwords and pass phrases, choose short passwords and pass phrases, and use variations on name, address, telephone numbers, and account names as passwords or pass phrases.

One 1990 study showed that a computer using standard dictionaries to guess passwords and pass phrases identified 3% of all the passwords on the systems being tested in fifteen minutes and 21% in the first week of testing. Thereafter, results slowed dramatically and after one year of testing only about 25% of the passwords and pass phrases had been correctly identified.

Much of the solution to the problem of weak security due to end user password-related behavior comes down to educating end users about proper choice, use, and protection of passwords and pass phrases. Some of the more common recommendations to end users are:

1. Never use variations on account names, addresses, telephone numbers, spouse's names, children's names, pet's names, or favorite hobbies, and places to visit as passwords or pass phrases.

2. Never choose as passwords and pass phrases words or phrases from on-line or off-line dictionaries.

3. Never use pairings of common words as passwords or pass phrases.

4. Never use dictionary words or phrases spelled backwards for passwords or pass phrases.

5. Repeated character strings and strings of numeric digits should not be used as passwords or pass phrases.

6. Never use words or phrases from a foreign language as passwords or pass phrases because they too can be broken or discovered via a computerized guessing program.

Having read the above list of Don'ts for password and pass phrase selection, you may be wondering what a good or hard to guess password or pass phrase looks like. The answer is that a good or hard to guess password or pass phrase:

1. Is long perhaps, as long as 16 characters or more.

2. Use mixtures of upper- and lowercase letters and symbols.

3. Use mixtures of letters, numeric digits, and punctuation marks.

If you do all that and can remember it, you've chosen a good password or pass phrase in the sense that it will take a while for a computer guessing program to guess your choice. Here's a good example:

summerisALMOSThere12..,

Some companies routinely run password guesser programs against their extranets. This procedure has two advantages namely it gives systems and network administrators some sense of how secure or not secure their extranet really is and it notifies end users who have chosen easy to guess passwords that they need to choose a tougher to guess password.

Another way to enhance extranet security is to require use of a password generator by end users. These programs often present to the end user a list of passwords that meet local security standards and from which the end user must choose his or her password or request that a new list of passwords to choose from be generated. Several rounds of password list generation may be required because many of the passwords that are excellent from the standpoint of security are very difficult for human beings to remember.

Many end users will want to choose a password that is easy to remember. Hard to remember passwords and pass phrases tend to get written down and taped to desks and terminals thereby creating yet another security weakness.

Password changer programs also exist that can block or prevent an end user from choosing a password or pass phrase that violates some of the more basic rules of choosing good passwords but which do not insist that end users choose hard to remember passwords. For example, a password changer program might insist that an end user choose at least a 16 character password but allow the end user to choose any 16 characters not all the same that he or she wishes to choose.

Password aging programs are also a solution to extranet authentication problems because they force extranet end users to periodically change their passwords and pass phrases to new ones. When the preselected age of a password or pass phrase expires, the end user must select a new one the next time that he or she logs in or be denied access to the system. Eventually, if a new password or pass phrase is not selected, the account will be disabled so that a call to the help desk or network administrator will be required for the end user to get back on-line. Good password aging programs also keep track of an end user's password selection history so that an end user cannot keep choosing the one, two, or three passwords and pass phrases over and over again. Naturally, the password history must be stored in a protected or encrypted form so that it cannot itself be stolen.

Yet another way to strengthen password-based authentication is by storing passwords in a special shadow password file or database known only to super users. The records and files where passwords and pass phrases are normally stored are filled with dummy values that cannot result from hashing passwords. Instead, the real hashed passwords and pass phrases are stored in a separate file or database where the super user can find them. Login and password programs must be modified to find and use shadow passwords. The theory of shadow passwords is that the bad guys will not know where to look for and how to find the real passwords.

Challenge response procedures make it possible for a host machine to verify that an end user knows his or her password or pass phrases without actually sending it over the wire to the host machine. This protects the password or pass phrase from anyone eavesdropping on the network.

Under a challenge response procedure, when a host receives a login request it responds by sending a challenge string of characters to the end user. The end user's machine responds to the challenge string by adding the end user's password to the string, hashing the whole thing, and sending it back to the host machine. The host performs a similar calculation on the end user's stored password and compares the result of its calculation to what it receives back from the end user. If there is a match, authentication occurs. The end user's password never crosses the wires to the host in the clear or human readable form so it can never be stolen from the network by eavesdroppers. However, the host machine has to store and/or be able to calculate the end user's password in hashed form so that it can compare it to the response string from the end user's machine.

One-time password technology and procedures can be used to overcome many of the security weaknesses in password systems that have been discussed in the above paragraphs. One-time passwords systems strengthen security because even if the one-time password is stolen by eavesdroppers on the network this will not help them because the stolen password will never be used again for authentication purposes. A one-time password system uses an end user's secret password to generate a collection of passwords each of which will be used once and only once for authentication.

To generate a list of one-time passwords an end user logs into a client machine or terminal with secure communication wires to a host machine and enters a secret password that is sent in human readable form across the wires to the host. The host machine responds by generating a list of one-time passwords, a sequence number, and a seed number. Next time, the end user attempts to log into the host, he or she will be asked to provide a one-time password corresponding to the sequence number and from the list of one-time passwords provided earlier by the host machine. Actually, the end user can regenerate the list of one-time passwords whenever he or she wants to on another computer with the right software by entering his or her secret password and seed. Every time the end user attempts authentication, he or she will enter the next password in sequence from his or her list of one-time passwords until the list is exhausted. When the list of one-time passwords is exhausted, the end user has to establish another secure communication link to the host and generate a new list of one-time passwords.

One-time passwords can also be generated with handheld hardware and software devices sometimes called handheld authenticators, password generators, and/or token generators. Synchronous, handheld authenticators produce a one-time password upon user request using an internal clock to generate the seed. Asynchronous, handheld authenticators respond to a challenge string from a host machine that an end user enters into them.

The response string appears on the authenticator's display, and the end user has to enter the displayed information into the host machine. Both asynchronous and synchronous handheld authenticators can themselves be made secure by requiring that an end user enter a personal identification number into them before using them. For handheld authenticators to work, both the handheld authenticators and host machines must agree on a common algorithm for generating one-time passwords and pass phrases. Smart cards operate very much like hand held authenticators but communicate directly with host machines themselves.

Handheld authenticators are becoming less expensive and more rugged and can make a significant contribution to enhancing extranet security through their support for one-time password systems. Currently these devices are available for less than fifty dollars when purchased in large quantities.

So far, this discussion of authentication technologies and procedures has focused on "two party trust" models of authentication. In a two party trust model, the end user machine or client submits its credentials to the host machine and assumes that the host machine really is the host machine that the end user wants to talk to and is not an impostor.

In addition, the host machine trusts that the client submitting credentials is in fact a valid client if its credentials validate. Thus, both parties namely the host machine and client machine trust each other based upon some criteria or no criteria at all in a two party trust model of authentication.

There is another model for authentication technologies and procedures known as a "third party trust" model of authentication. In this model, both the host and the client machine rely upon a trusted third party called a "key distribution center" to vouch for each other. Neither the client nor the host machine trust each other but they both trust what the key distribution center says about the other. The key distribution center treats both host and client machines exactly the same way during the authentication process namely as "principals." For example, when an end user logs in, the end user or client machine contacts the key distribution center and requests credentials that it can present to the host machine that it wants to access. The key distribution center responds to this request by sending the requested credentials in a doubly or twice encrypted form. The client machine must be able to undo the second encryption in order to present the requested credentials to the host machine that it wants to access. If the client machine cannot undo the second encryption, it cannot present valid credentials. When it receives valid credentials from the client machine, the host machine undoes the first encryption using its password and knows that the end user's client machine is what it claims to be. Authentication has now occurred.

If third party trust models are to provide strong security, the key distribution centers must be a well protected and a highly secure system. Thus, key distribution centers are usually kept in physically secure rooms and serviced at their consoles and not over a network. Furthermore, key distribution centers usually only run programs directly related to the key distribution function and nothing else.

Likewise, key distribution centers are usually backed up locally and never over a network unless the bit stream is encrypted. Back up tapes need to be physically protected if not encrypted. The database containing each principals secret password needs to be encrypted with a key and process known only to security administrators and the key distribution software.

Unfortunately, these requirements make third party trust models of authentication difficult to implement for extranets. Thus, if a cracker manages to breach a key distribution center, all of its principals are immediately at risk. The key distribution center is a single point of failure for the network so additional synchronized key distribution centers are required as back ups or credentials need to be locally cached until the failed key distribution center can be brought back on-line. Moreover, key distribution centers lack scalability because their scope is limited to clients and servers willing to trust them. This fact usually implies some type of local environment like a college campus.

However, possibly the greatest drawback to third party trust models and key distribution centers from the standpoint of extranets is the fact that key distribution centers need to be serviced and managed locally and not over the network. This can be expensive and difficult to do in the case of a global extranet. It is difficult to synchronize local key distribution center management and administration across the globe.

Host to host authentication is just as important from a security standpoint as is end user to host authentication. Thus host machines need to determine whether or not it is safe to accept packets of data from other host machines, whether or not it is safe to accept operating system updates from other host machines, whether or not it is safe to accept "host unreachable messages" as valid, and whether or not it is safe to export files and software to other host machines. The general state of the art on the Internet today is that no authentication process at all occurs between host machines. If one host machine believes that another host machine's IP address is valid, it trusts that machine. However, IP addresses are easily obtained and faked with no authentication process required. Since the Internet's Domain Naming System permits a one to many mapping of names to host machines, host names likewise provide no basis for authentication or security either.

Some host to host protocols do permit weak authentication procedures in the sense that passwords are exchanged in human readable form as part of the protocol exchange that occurs between host machines. Thus, a cracker would have to eavesdrop on the network in order to steal host passwords and breach security.

Host to host security just like end user to end user security can be made much stronger through the use of public and private key encryption procedures. These procedures are required for secure end to end tunneling and are described next.

Cryptographic Solutions to the Extranet Security Challenge

"Cryptology" is the science of secret communications. The two branches or major subdivisions of cryptology are "cryptography" or the science of making and keeping communications secret and "cryptanalysis" or the science of discovering or breaking secret communications.

"Encryption" refers to the process of converting communications from human readable to some type of nonhuman readable form. "Decryption" refers to the process of converting communications from nonhuman readable form back to human readable form. Human readable communications or data is usually referred to as "plaintext" and nonhuman readable communications or data is usually referred to as "ciphertext."

Encryption and decryption processes and algorithms can be used to create digital signatures that uniquely identify the authorship of a message. An encrypted message itself plus a key provided by the author or a trusted third party can be used to decrypt the message and thereby prove both that the message was not altered and was encrypted by the author. If this were not so, the receiver would not be able to decrypt the message with the author's key.

A "key" is a word, value, or whatever that must be input along with the secret message into the decryption process in order to decrypt the ciphertext. It turns out that the length of the key or the size of the key space from which the key was selected has a critical impact on the strength of the protection provided by the encryption process. This is because in general the longer the key and thus the size of the key space from which the key was chosen, the harder it will be for a computer to decrypt or decipher the secret message by guessing the key. The key is a critical part of both the encryption and decryption processes. The key need not necessarily be the same for both of these processes. Different keys may be used.

There are two basic types of cryptographic systems in wide use today namely secret key and public key systems. In a secret key system, the same key is used for both the encryption and decryption processes and the sender must share the secret key along with the encrypted message with the receiver of the encrypted message. Thus security is critically dependent on the ability of the sender and receiver to exchange and to keep secret keys as well as messages. Since exactly the same key is used to encrypt and to decrypt messages, private or secret key systems are often called "symmetric" cryptographic systems.

Public key cryptographic systems use two different keys, which just like one-time passwords cannot be derived or calculated from each other. Thus one of the keys usually the key used for encryption can be made public. A message encrypted with this "public key" can only be decrypted with the secret or private key and thus cannot be read by anyone who does not have the private key. Because different keys are used for encryption and decryption, public private key cryptosystems are often referred to as "asymmetric" systems.

Obviously, both secret key and public key cryptosystems require secure key management in order to effectively provide secure communications. Thus, with secret key systems the sender and the receiver of a secure communication must exchange or agree upon a secret key, which can be difficult if the sender and receiver are far apart. With a public key system, something or someone must establish that the public key really and truly does belong to its alleged owner. This is usually done in one of two ways either a trusted third party known as a certification authority vouches for the ownership of a public key or someone you know and trust vouches for the ownership of the public key. This latter procedure is sometimes called a "web of trust or transitive trust."

There are several different factors that determine just how strong and effective a crytosystem is. These factors include how secret the keys are, absence of back doors or ways to subvert the encryption, decryption processes by workarounds, and resistance to guessing or other forms of brute force attack. Cryptosystems that incorporate proprietary encryption and decryption algorithms are often viewed with suspicion by experts because such systems are not subject to ongoing review and testing by cryptographic experts. Such experts use a variety of techniques to test the strength of cryptosystems including brute force attempts to guess the encryption and decryption keys by running computer programs that examine the entire key space and test the results with plaintext and ciphertext. The experts may start with ciphertext only and try to determine the plaintext or start with plaintext only and try to match samples of ciphertext or choose the next message to be encrypted based upon the results obtained by attempting to encrypt the previous message, etc.

Modern cryptographic theory says that with one exception given enough time and computer resources any cryptographic system can be broken although it may take a very, very long time to break the system. The one exception is a one-time or one-time pad system in which a new and truly random key is used once and only once to encrypt and decrypt a message. Since the randomly chosen bits of the key are combined with the plaintext via something called an "exclusive or operation," the resulting bits of the ciphertext are random and impossible to decrypt without the one-time key. Although this process is highly interesting from the stand point of theory, it is very impractical in that the key management and exchange issues become extremely challenging. Thus, such systems are not yet suitable for extranets.

One-way hash functions are widely used to store passwords and for other purposes related to network and computer security. A hash function takes plain text as input, compresses it into a shorter message, and converts it to a nonhuman readable form. The output of the hash function is a message checksum or message integrity check value that can be used to verify the integrity of the message. The message checksum acts as a unique fingerprint that can be used to identify a message. One-way hash functions are preferred for computer and network security because the output of a one-way hash function cannot be reversed to regenerate the original human readable message. In general, the longer the hash value the harder it is for an attacker to reverse or break it by guesswork or other types of brute force attacks.

Some of the more popular hash algorithms are MD2 or message digest 2 which was designed for use with Privacy Enhanced Mail and produces 128 bit hash values. MD2 has been successfully broken by cryptanalysis. It is byte oriented and requires a multiple of 16 bytes as input. MD2 will pad the message as necessary with a multiple of 16 bytes in order to satisfy the 16 byte requirement.

▶ MD4 or message digest 4 also produces 128 bit hash values but is optimized for 32 bit register machines like Intel's newer line of processors. This means that MD4 runs faster than MD2. MD4 also requires 64 bytes of padding rather than 16.

▶ MD5 or message digest 5 is the newer, more secure, extended, and slightly slower version of MD4 which was never broken but began to look like it might be broken soon. MD5 extensions are meant to overcome the weaknesses found in MD4 by cryptanalysis.

▶ SHA or secure hash algorithm was developed by the National Security Agency and the National Institute of Standards and Technology in an effort to strengthen MD4 in ways different from the similar effort made in MD5. For example, SHA generates relatively long (160 bit) hash values.

There are other hash algorithms as well and new ones being invented all the time as part of ongoing efforts to improve information security. Most modern cryptosystems and related algorithms are based on advanced mathematical techniques especially advanced number theory. The list given below briefly summarizes some of the more common encryption and decryption algorithms that are likely to be used today to enhance Internet, intranet, and extranet security.

▶ DES or the Data Encryption Standard was proposed by IBM and adopted by the federal government in 1977 as the standard algorithm for encryption and decryption of commercial and sensitive but unclassified government information. Although the original life time of DES was expected to be five to ten years, it is still in use today more than twenty years later. DES has been very effective in that twenty years of extensive cryptanalysis have failed to break the standard. However, DES is reaching the end of its life in the sense that it is estimated that a one million dollar computer in today's prices could break DES by brute force guessing or searching of the entire DES key space in less than a day.

▶ TDES or triple DESs are modern versions of DES with enhancements designed to strengthen the security of the original DES system. In one version of TDES, two different keys are used to alternately encrypt an decrypt data. The use of two different keys in effect substantially increases the key space and doubles the effective key length to 112 bits making it much harder to break the algorithm by guessing the keys used. Since DES encryption and decryption processes are exactly the same except for the fact that different keys are used for each, successive rounds of decryption and encryption with different keys used a specific order amounts to increased rounds of encryption and better security. Thus a triple round of encryption, decryption, and encryption with two different keys used in a specific order is very hard to break. If the two keys used are exactly the same then the TDES process has exactly the same result as a single application of the DES process. Thus, the same machine can implement both DES and TDES without modification to its hardware.

▶ IDEA or the International Data Encryption Algorithm was originally invented by private European cryptologists. Some people who do not trust governments or government agencies consider the fact that IDEA did not originate from a government source to be a plus. IDEA uses a 128 bit key and is streamlined for implementation in software. IDEA is still fairly new but it has so far resisted attempts to break it.

▶ Diffie-Hellman allows both the sender and receiver of information to derive keys for encryption and decryption without requiring them to exchange keys. Thus, this algorithm overcomes a major security weakness of secret key systems namely that the sender and receiver must agree on the use of a common key. When using the Diffie-Hellman algorithm, each person selects a large number of 512 bits. These large numbers are then shared or exchanged by the sender and receiver each of whom randomly selects a secret 512 bit number and mathematically combines it with his or her first number. The results are shared between the sender and receiver, and each performs another calculation with the other person's number. What comes out of the final calculation is the same for both people namely a secret key which they can both use for encryption and decryption purposes.

▶ RSA or the Rivest, Shamir, and Adelman cryptosystem is the first public key cryptosystem to offer encryption as well as digital signature functionality. It is the most widely used cryptosystem today on the Internet, intranets, and elsewhere. (Actually the most widely used security system in use today on the Internet, intranets, and extranets may be no system at all, but this is changing rapidly.) The basis of RSA security rests upon a widely believed but unproven mathematical assumption or conjecture namely that it is extremely difficult to factor the product of two numbers each of which has 100 or so digits in it. It is important to note that although it is difficult to factor a product of large numbers, it is not impossible. In April 1994, a 129 digit number was successfully factored into 64 and 65 digit prime numbers after using eight months and 5,000 MIP years of computer cycles. These large numbers along with some number theory are used to generate public and private key pairs that can be used for encryption and decryption. Anything encrypted with the public key can only be decrypted with the private key, and anything encrypted with the private key can only be decrypted with the public key. RSA requires significant computer power for implementation and therefore is often used to complement less computationally intensive cryptosystems by encrypting their keys only rather than entire messages. The receiver of a message uses RSA to decrypt a key and then applies the key and a different cryptosystem to decrypt the message received.

▶ RSA can also be used to encrypt hash values with a sender's private key. The recipient of a message decrypts the hash value with the sender's public key and then computes a new hash value on the message. If the computed and decrypted hash values match then the recipient knows that the message arrived unchanged and was sent by the owner of the public key used to decrypt the hash value.

▶ Skipjack was developed by the National Security Agency cryptologists as an intended replacement for DES. It is intended to be used to protect unclassified data and to be implemented in special hardware in order to deter reverse software engineering attacks on it. Not very much is known or likely to be known about it given the government's desire to keep cryptographic information secret.

▶ Clipper is the name of the special hardware chip that implements Skipjack and is intended to secure any kind of data being sent over digital voice communication lines. Clipper has a back door that permits law enforcement agencies to obtain the session key that a clipper chip uses to secure a communication connection or session. Different keys are used for different sessions. When manufactured, each Clipper chip is designed to hold a unique secret key and identification number. Both of these are required to communicate with another Clipper chip and to create a Law Enforcement Access Field or LEAF that accompanies encrypted data.

▶ LEAF indicates which key is needed to unravel the secret session keys also contained in the Clipper chip. Two different federal agencies will each know one half of the secret session keys and in theory would not reveal them to law enforcement agencies without court order or other legal justification. Whether or not you feel that you can trust such a system probably depends upon how much you feel that you can trust government not to abuse its powers. Current proposals call for the Department of the Treasury and the National Institute of Standards and Technology to be the key escrow agents.

As you can see from the above discussion of cryptographic algorithms DES, TDES, IDEA, and RSA are the security procedures that you most likely use or meet when implementing extranets. However, if you are implementing a global extranet, you need to be aware of the United States export restrictions that apply to cryptographic technologies. In fact, the United States government classifies this technology as a "munition" and regulates its export as heavily or may be even more heavily than it regulates the export of munitions. The U.S. government does not want one of its enemies to implement secret codes that it cannot break. Thus, those wishing to export this technology have to work closely with the United States government and the Department of State in order to do so.

Actually, much of the most modern and innovative cryptographic theory and algorithms like RSA and IDEA that come from private sources are broadly published and understood. However, it is illegal to export hardware and software that implements these and other algorithms to many countries. The United States government sometimes allows exceptions for encryption used for authentication systems but not for information exchange. Thus, software that implements digital signatures may be exportable under an exception process. Sometimes export is allowed if the encryption and decryption keys are not more than 40 bits in length. Obviously, anyone implementing an extranet that crosses international borders and who is concerned with security and cryptosystems needs to consult legal experts in technology export laws. In addition, many countries restrict the use of cryptosystems by any and all private citizens and companies. Thus, legal experts in the local use of this technology should be consulted as well.

Firewall Solutions to the Extranet Security Challenge

The use of firewalls to manage Internet, intranet, and extranet security is exploding in popularity. Firewalls are collections of filters and gateways or protocol translators that shield a trusted network within a fence or perimeter from untrusted networks. Thus, firewalls represent the boundary or moat around a trusted network.

Packet filter firewalls function by examining the header of each packet of information arriving at the firewall. The packet filter firewall then applies a set of firewall rules to the header information to decide whether or not to let the packet pass through the firewall from an untrusted network to a trusted network. The order in which the rules are applied is crucial because the first rule met which permits or blocks passage of a packet decides the fate of that packet. Often, different rules apply to packets moving from trusted to untrusted networks versus packets moving from untrusted to trusted networks. If the header information in a packet does not map to any packet filtering rule, then the packet is generally blocked and does not pass through the firewall. Packet filters or screening routers often come bundled with router software and can be implemented by configuring and setting up the router. Screening routers usually operate at the IP layer with only occasional looks at the transport layer of the TCP/IP network protocol.

Screening routers and packet filters offer a wide variety of functionality that can be extremely useful for enhancing extranet security. For example, these routers can be configured to block all incoming traffic from specified external networks and other sources, to permit only incoming SMTP traffic to pass through the firewall, and to allow outbound but not inbound Telnet sessions.

The proper configuration of screening routers and packet filters requires understanding of what action to take with regard to packets (i.e., blocking or passing), the protocol layer at which filtering of packets occurs (i.e., internetworking or transmission control), source Internetworking

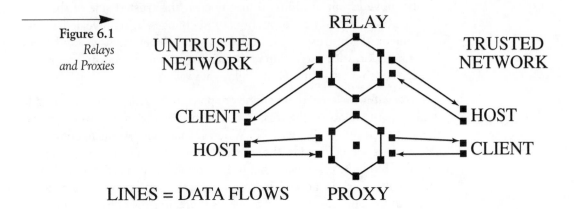

Figure 6.1
*Relays
and Proxies*

Protocol addresses, destination Internetworking Protocol addresses, source port numbers for Transmission Control Protocol, destination port numbers for Transmission Control Protocol, and flags for Transmission Control Protocol, or options for Internetworking Protocol. As you can see from this list, the setting up of screening router or packet filter rules requires a detailed and specific knowledge of networking.

Application gateways can be used to increase extranet security by applying rules to the application layer of the network. Application gateways come in three distinct flavors namely relays, proxies, and server filters (see Note 6.1).

NOTE 6.1 ————————————▶

   Types of Firewalls
   TCP/IP layers
   Application, network, transport   →   Application level gateways
   Link, physical   →   Packet level gateways

Relay gateways contribute the least to greater extranet security because they simply pass data back and forth between client and server. Their function is triggered by the initial client connect to the server and their intent is to accomplish delivery and receipt of data only. Relay gateways are useful because application services can be placed behind a relay gateway and moved around the trusted side of the network without revealing anything about the network addresses or architecture behind the relay gateway to clients or servers on the untrusted side of the network. Data freely passes back and forth across the relay gateway, but the application can be moved from machine to machine on the trusted side of the network without any address or architectural changes being revealed to any machine on the untrusted side of the network. Relay gateways can be run in conjunction with server filters to increase extranet security and to log all accesses that pass through the relay gateway.

Proxy gateways are either generic or application aware. They are usually used to assist clients on the trusted side of the network to access servers on the untrusted side of the network. When such a client wants to communicate with a server outside the trusted network, it begins by opening a channel to the proxy gateway that uses a proxy specific protocol to identify the actual server's location. The proxy gateway then establishes a connection with the remote server and proceeds thereafter to act like a relay gateway to the client and the server. It can implement a limited form of access control by restricting access based upon client and server identifiers.

Application aware proxy gateways are servers that are fully aware of application level protocols. For example, a File Transfer Protocol proxy gateway implements the file transfer protocol and a Telnet proxy gateway implements a Telnet protocol.

Unfortunately, application aware proxy gateways usually require unique source code that is not reusable in proxy gateways for other applications. Because of their application level awareness, application aware proxy gateways can be used to prevent users from doing things that make no sense in light of the applications that they are running. Thus, application aware proxy gateways can be used to prevent users from doing uploads when downloads are the only actions that make sense, say in the case of running FTP only.

Server filters or host-based firewalls are yet another form of security device that can be used to increase the overall security of extranets. These filters operate at the application layer and operate very differently from the packet filters that operate at the lower layers of the network protocol. Thus at the application level most of the filtering is based upon source and destination addresses and port numbers. All of the packet level information of flags and packets and so forth is lost at the application level. Logging of connections, disconnections, and sessions is normally implemented along with filtering by server filters. Most of the actual access decisions by the server filter are based upon a client list of clients along with network addresses and host names that are known to be valid or invalid.

Required Architectural and Tunneling Tradeoffs

As you can see from the above discussion, firewalls can be useful devices for increasing extranet security because a single firewall can be used to manage the security of many devices. Without a firewall, network managers would have to manage the security of each and every device on the network separately. This would be impossible in the case of networks with thousands of devices on them.

However, firewalls can make their contribution to increased extranet security only if they can examine the packets of information, the source and destination network addresses, or the source and destination port numbers of the information flowing past them.

This is not a problem if an extranet or virtual private network tunnel starts and stops at a firewall. However, this is a big problem if an extranet or virtual private network tunnel stretches from desktop to desktop. In the latter case, all of the information passing the firewall will be encrypted and the firewall will not be able to apply some types of filtering rules unless it first decrypts the information which violates the very idea of a secure and private desktop to desktop extranet connection. Unfortunately, there is no way around this problem. Tradeoffs will have to be made. If a secure desktop to desktop extranet is desired, some of the network security provided by firewalls will in fact be lost.

Some Ethical and Product Solutions

The issue of prior consent is critical to the public perception of extranet security. Extranet users want to know what kind of information about them is being gathered and how that information will be used. Often extranet users are quite comfortable about sharing information provided that they have been given a chance to give or withhold prior consent.

In fact, groups like Truste are recommending that merchants post their information gathering and sharing practices to their web sites so that extranet users can decide ahead of time whether or not they wish to participate given the stated information practices and ethics of that web site. Compliant web sites are often marked with the "Truste" symbol. The posting of information ethics practices to web sites and abiding by such ethical practices can go a long way toward increasing extranet user trust and reducing or eliminating negative perceptions of extranet security.

Often consumers are happy to fill out registration forms for contests giving all sorts of marketing information about themselves in order to have a chance to win free stuff. This is especially true if consumers are told up front how the information on them will be used and whether or not it will be sold or passed on to others.

P3P is a standard supported by MIT's World Wide Web Consortium. It requires up front disclosure of the business practices and recognizes consumer choices in the how the information gathered on them is used by merchants. P3P helps merchants and consumers avoid a mismatch of security standards and puts the consumer in charge of how information gathered on them will be used.

Increasingly, there is software available like cookie crumblers that remove unwanted cookies or software that allows merchants to track the buying preferences and web site visits of consumers from the hard drives of extranet user's client machines. Even without cookie crumbler software, extranet users can search their hard drives for cookies and remove them. Both Netscape and Microsoft are building consumer preferences into new browser software so that consumers can control the amount of information gathered on them. This new software functionality allows the user to opt in or out of tracking by click streams and cookies.

For more information on these and other security and privacy standards and solutions take a look at:

http://www.narrowline.com

http://www.neodata.com

http://www.truste.org

http://www.w3c.org

Summary of Solutions for Extranet Security

The following table summarizes some of the solutions and mechanisms for increasing extranet security. Many of these solutions are undergoing rapid

Table 6.4 *Meeting the Extranet Security Challenge*

Security Solution	Pluses for Extranet Security	Negatives for Extranet Security
Security Policy Guidelines	Establishes and communicates goals and direction for security	Guidelines will be resisted by creative technical people if they are perceived to be edicts.
Security Policy Actions	Establishes and communicates actions to enhance extranet security	Tradeoffs will need to be considered as multiple and somewhat conflicting actions may be required.
Authentication with passwords or pass phrases	Most end users are familiar with passwords and pass phrases	It is hard to choose and remember strong passwords or pass phrases. However, password generation programs and renewal programs can help overcome this limitation.
Token Cards	Token cards are inexpensive and convenient to use	Although these cards can be lost or loaned, they are effective when combined with other security techniques.
Biometric Devices	Sometimes capable of identifying individual end users	Expensive and prone to errors due to tolerance margins.

Table 6.4 *Meeting the Extranet Security Challenge (Continued)*

Security Solution	Pluses for Extranet Security	Negatives for Extranet Security
Cryptographic solutions	These are increasingly powerful and effective	Not everyone has the software to implement these and there are legal restrictions on their use.
Firewall solutions	These are increasingly powerful and effective	These solutions require detailed knowledge of the network for successful implementation and constant logging and perusing of access logs in order to be effective. Their use may be incompatible with implementation of desktop to desktop tunneling architectures.

development so the table is neither complete nor final, but it will make you aware of at least some of the solutions available for increasing extranet security.

Example of a Product Solution

Unfortunately, good security can be expensive to implement. However the prices of security products are dropping rapidly as security technology advances. For example, Internet Scanner 5.0 from Internet Security Systems (see the article "Security Crackdown" [Shotland and Taschek, March 1998]) will scan the network for breaches of security as well as potential security risks. This product and others like it are exciting because they include a large number of security checks and improved reporting features, trend analysis, and the ability to drop security reports into any ODBC compliant database. All of this is available for about $2,700 for a 30-node license.

Although network monitoring is only part of a security solution, it is an important part whose technology has been improving rapidly. Even though it is often difficult to cite a specific percentage of a web site's budget that should be devoted to meeting security needs because of all of the variables involved, Don Elledge, manager of the Distributed Computing

Infrastructure Group at DeLoitte & Touche LLP, as quoted in Daniel P. Dern's article "Protect or Serve" (April 1997), suggests that 10 to 15 percent is not unreasonable. This article goes on to give some excellent cost and sizing information for implementing secure web sites at InsWeb, Pennsylvania State University, and The Internet Company.

For more product information look at James Taschek's article, "Taking the Internet Private" (Jan. 1998), for pricing and comparison of extranet security products priced from $3,995 for a hardware firewall to $995 for a server plus ten client tunneling software package. Product pricing is often determined by the number of protocols, tunnels, nodes, access controls, and key management functions provided.

Chapter Summary

In this chapter, we've explored the social concerns with information privacy and security as well as the management and policy issues raised by these concerns. We've also explored specific technical solutions to the challenges presented by extranet security issues. It is important to remember that extranet security is really an enabler of greater use of extranets by everyone and of electronic commerce over extranets.

Without both better security and the public perception of better security greater use of extranets and electronic commerce over extranets will suffer. The following items were explored in detail in this chapter and, in fact, make up a useful checklist of items to consider in designing and architecting solutions to the many challenges of extranet security.

► Increasingly widespread social concerns with the confidentiality, integrity, and availability of information.

► The meaning of the words "extranet security."

► Examples of extranet information security policy guidelines and of extranet information security actions in light of the security, management, and administration challenges of personal web sites.

► Authentication with passwords or pass phrases, token cards, and biometric devices.

► Cryptographic solutions to the extranet security challenge.

► Firewall solutions to the extranet security challenge.

► Architectural and tunneling tradeoffs required to overcome the extranet security challenge.

▶ Some ethical and product solutions to the extranet security challenge.

▶ Example of a product solution.

▶ A summary of solutions for extranet security.

   I am optimistic that security challenges being posed by extranets are being solved both by the adoption and posting of information use standards, the adoption of technical security standards, and by the introduction of new hardware and software security products.

7

Extranet Performance

Chapter Objectives

The objectives of this chapter are to explore solutions to many of the performance problems and issues commonly experienced when implementing and using extranets. Much of our discussion focuses on the performance problems associated with the readiness of the Internet to move audio and visual files over the net because the movement of audio and visual files pushes the performance boundaries of the Internet and therefore of extranets as well. There is really nothing special about audio/visual files other than the fact that their typically large size makes predictable and acceptable performance over the extranet a challenge.

Moreover, the movement of audio/visual files across the Internet and extranets is an urgent need in the television, movie, and broadcast industries. Today these industries spend large amounts of money on human carriers to move video and audiotape from content creators and editors to content broadcasters. Even more importantly, these industries often lose large amounts of money when they cannot meet broadcast deadlines at least partly because of the time that it takes human carriers to move content from location to location.

Ease of connectivity to the Internet, use of standards, and multivendor support are some of the strengths of the extranet for audio/visual transfer. However, predictability of performance and quality remains a weakness. Audio/visual technologies are major tools for collaboration over the extranet.

Perhaps more importantly from an extranet perspective, better audio/visual technology is needed to promote extranet commerce. This is because many business people as well as consumers are unwilling to purchase based purely on textual product descriptions. They want to see and hear and maybe even touch some kinds of product before they buy them.

Better audio/visual technology is on its way and will enable commerce like real time auctions over an extranet.

This chapter covers:

▶ The relationship between usage and performance.

▶ Some performance requirements for moving and displaying large audio/visual files.

▶ Some discussion of the lack of predictability and limitations of store and forward and routing systems for moving large audio/visual files across the extranet, especially in real time.

▶ Some end to end and desktop to desktop solutions and requirements for moving large audio/visual files.

▶ Some file compression solutions and requirements for moving large audio/visual files.

▶ Some tools solutions and requirements for moving and displaying large audio/visual files.

▶ A proposed solution from providers of proprietary WAN-based network services to the performance predictability and the quality predictability problems of the extranet.

▶ The fast server solution to the audio/visual collaborative computing performance problem.

▶ The gateway solution to the computing performance problems of the extranet.

▶ A best performance investment.

Video on demand and audio/visual collaborative computing over the Internet are two of the hottest areas of research and development today. There is an explosion of products being brought to the market to support collaborative computing over the Internet and extranet including but not limited to Communique from InSoft, ProShare from Intel, In Person from Silicon Graphics, and PictureTel from Compression Labs. The Association for Computing Machinery and Institute of Electrical and Electronic Engineers publish research in this area. Much of this research is aimed at developing new file compression technologies to overcome the performance limitations of the extranet. I cover some of these new compression technologies in this chapter.

The Relationship Between Usage and Performance

In many ways extranet usage and Internet commerce usage statistics are conceptually similar to the waterfall model discussed in many books on software development and engineering. This is because, of the thousands of hits to any given web server, only a tiny percentage actually come from users interested in finding product or services information. Of those users only a very small percentage are willing to complete a template describing their interests in products and services and only a tiny percentage of those who fill out templates are actually willing to buy anything. Note 7.1 summarizes this situation.

NOTE 7.1 ━━━━━━━━━━▶

The Extranet Usage Waterfall

Total hits = 7000

Product hits = 210

Template hits = 32

Orders = ?

The implications of this for extranet performance are profound. One company was very successful in attracting traffic and hits to its sports page. As the traffic and hits to its sports page increased, overall extranet performance decreased due to the heavy load on the network. By studying usage statistics, this company found that the users visiting its sports page rarely requested product or services information, completed and returned templates, or bought anything. In fact, the company improved extranet performance and improved sales by turning off its sports page.

It is becoming easier and easier to collect user statistics and profiles. A "cookie" is a user identifier placed on a browser by a server the first time a time new user visits the server. Whenever that user visits the server thereafter, the server will receive the cookie and build a profile of that user's interests and preferences. The business owning the server can use this information to aim special ads and promotions at the user. Unless the user knows where to look for the cookie files stored on his or her browser and deletes them automatically via software or manually or unless the server decides to limit the lifetime of its cookies, this will process will continue indefinitely. Figure 7.1 shows an example of the cookie dialogue between a server and browsers.

The implication of all of this for solving extranet performance problems is that dramatic extranet performance improvements may be possible by

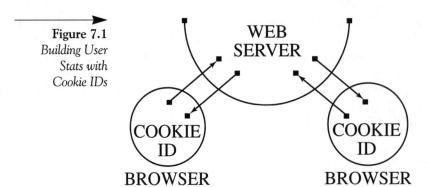

Figure 7.1
*Building User
Stats with
Cookie IDs*

understanding and acting upon usage statistics. This understanding and action can even be fully automated. *Redirection* as illustrated in Figure 7.2 is an example of this. Redirection occurs when there are two geographically dispersed servers that contain identical content. Sometimes a user very close to one of the servers will make a request to the much more remote content server simply because the user does not know of its companion server. If the remote server is smart enough to sense this, it can improve extranet performance and decrease the user's time to content simply by redirecting the request to the server closer to the user.

Understanding where the different parts of an image come from that an end user receives when requesting content from an extranet is also key to resolving performance issues. For example, many web pages and even some extranet web pages include advertising banners that come from different servers when the page is actually downloaded to a user's browser. Thus, a user may find themselves in a situation where most of the content of a requested page is downloaded quickly but the banner or graphic takes

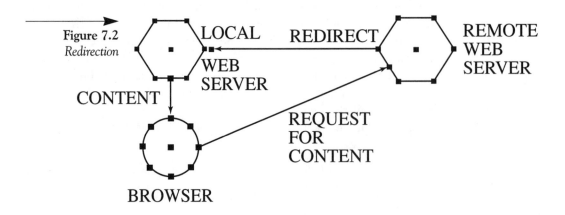

Figure 7.2
Redirection

a long time to download because unknown to the user that part of the page is coming from a separate server. There have been cases where banners have been shut off or different suppliers found in order to improve performance of an extranet and an end user's time to download an entire page.

Performance Requirements for Moving Large Audio/Visual Files

Table 7.1 *Speed and Bandwidth Requirements for Moving and Viewing Large Audio/Visual Files*

Function	Speed Required for Real-Time Delivery	Speed Currently Available over the Internet
Moving 30 Second Television Commercials*	1.5 Megabits/Minute	1.5 Megabits/Minute
Low-Quality Viewing and Listening	1.5 Megabits/Minute	1.5 Megabits/Minute
High-Quality Viewing and Listening	6–9 Megabits/Minute	1.5 Megabits/Minute
Very-High-Quality Viewing and Listening	90–100 Megabits/Minute	1.5 Megabits/Minute

Audio/Visual Files Based Upon 1995 Networld/Interop Discussions.
*Only very-low-quality broadcast is possible over the Internet today.

Lack of Predictability and Limitations of Routing Systems

The design goal of early store and forward systems was to effectively move relatively short text-based e-mail across the network. As a result of this design goal most store and forward systems were designed and implemented with disk and memory much too small to support large audio/visual files. This means that part or all of a large audio/visual file is likely to be lost or dropped as it hops across the network and encounters different store and forward computers without enough memory to store all or part of the file.

Store and forward systems also cause messages to hop from routing computer to routing computer. This is illustrated in Figure 7.3. The number of hops and transmission delays at each routing computer varies

Figure 7.3
*Store and
Forward Networks*

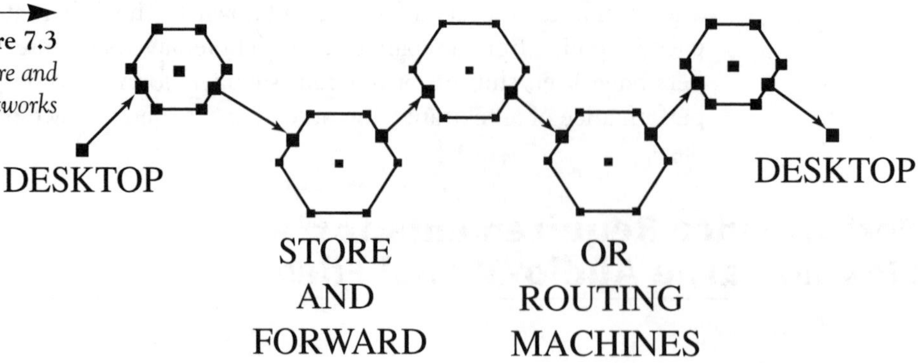

DESKTOP   DESKTOP

STORE   OR
AND   ROUTING
FORWARD   MACHINES

greatly and depends upon the amount of network traffic and congestion at each node of the network. This lack of predictability can mean that it can take hours and not just minutes to move a large audio/visual file across the network. The time delays in hoping from routing to routing computer make real-time data transfer across the extranet extremely difficult to achieve. In fact, this problem has steadily grown worse due to the growth of the Internet and improvements in disk storage capacity. These two factors have caused more and more data to be widely distributed across the network and increased transmission delays.

End to end or desktop to desktop delivery systems with different design goals and without the memory limitations of store and forward systems are needed to solve these problems. New hardware, software, and services will all be important elements of these end to end systems. See the discussion in the fast server solution section of this chapter for more discussion of what these emerging end to end systems may look like.

Some Solutions and Requirements for Moving Large Audio/Visual Files

Adoption of standards that support high-performance transfer of files across the Internet and tools to bridge the diversity of the desktop environments are elements of end to end solutions for moving audio/visual files across the extranet. Fast encryption/decryption tools, fast compression/decompression tools, remote system sensing tools, file encryption/decryption standards, and file compression/decompression standards are at the top of the list. Some of the newer compression/decompression algorithms and standards are listed in Note 7.2. The file encryption/decryption standards are discussed in the chapter on security and so will not be discussed here.

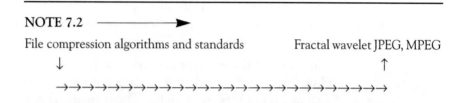

NOTE 7.2

File compression algorithms and standards   Fractal wavelet JPEG, MPEG

Slow scan is an important end to end solution to the performance challenge of the extranet. In fact, very slow scanning and frame viewing speeds reduce the extranet performance bottleneck and are perfectly adequate for observing the behavior and collaboration of your colleagues at a business meeting. The faster scanning and frame viewing speeds required for viewing movies or television are not required for many business and collaborative applications that span the extranet. Slow scan helps overcome some of the jitter and image jerkiness problems of video transmission over the extranet.

Some important products to remember that make use of some of these end to end solutions are CUCME, QuickTime, and ProShare Audio/Visual. Perhaps the classic end to end solution for the extranet is I phone or Internet phone which is a very low cost alternative to plain old long-distance telephone service.

Some File Compression Solutions and Requirements

There are two types of file compression algorithms available on the market today—namely those that actually throw away data when compressing the file and those that compress without destroying or throwing away any data. Both types of algorithms can be highly effective in compressing large audio/visual files. Some of the algorithms that throw away data are so effective that even after 90% of the information in a compressed file has been deleted the decompressed file is still viewable. Fractal, wavelet, and H.320 are some of the newer audio compression technologies and standards being introduced to the market today.

Algorithms are now being implemented into standards for moving different audio/visual file types. For example, MPEG and its older cousin JPEG are standards for moving and compressing audio/visual files. JPEG is platform dependent in the sense that JPEG files developed on a Macintosh will not run on a PC and vice versa and was originally designed to compress static images. MPEG is the newer standard that is platform independent, was originally designed to compress motion or dynamic images, and which compresses video files by as much as 90% by keeping only the differences between successive frames of the video and by throwing away the rest of the information.

In fact, MPEG incorporates some of the static image framework of JPEG. The MPEG standard is undergoing rapid development and there are now MPEG versions 1 and 2. These emerging standards should go a long way toward solving the performance limitations of the extranet with regard to moving large files over the net.

Some Tools, Solutions, and Requirements

End to end tools are urgently needed to make the extranet successful. A great end to end or desktop to desktop tool would look at the recipient's desktop before a sender sends an MPEG or other file type to the recipient and tell the sender whether or not the recipient's desktop has the software and hardware tools available that are necessary to open and view the MPEG or other file type being sent. This type of tool would dramatically improve audio/visual collaboration over the extranet. This is because one of the major performance limitations of the extranet today results from the variability of desktop environments in the sense that not every desktop has the decompression software necessary to decompress and view large audio/visual files.

Another set of tools that are necessary to improve the performance of the extranet are tools that enable the client system to retrieve files in the background while the user does other things in the foreground. This is important because of the relatively long time that it can take to retrieve a large audio/visual file. It can take more than an hour to retrieve such a file.

Annotation tools can also be used to successfully overcome the performance limitations of the extranet. These tools allow the user to edit and mark up audio/visual files and to send only the changes or annotations back across the extranet to the content developer (see Note 7.3). The entire file does not have to be sent back across the extranet to the original content developer. Annotation tools are likely to be especially valued by editors and reviewers.

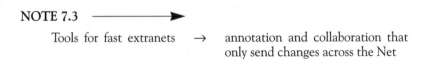

NOTE 7.3

Tools for fast extranets   →   annotation and collaboration that
only send changes across the Net

A Proposed Solution to the Bandwidth and Quality Control Predictability Problems

One of the more interesting solutions being proposed by providers of proprietary WAN-based services like the telephone companies is that users standardize on Internet and extranet technologies like TCP/IP, but use proprietary network common carriers to move their data because of the bandwidth control and quality control that these carriers can provide (see Figure 7.4).

The amount of caching or buffering of images to control jerkiness or jitter needed depends upon the reliability and predictability of the network backbone used. The more reliable and predictable the network backbone used the less buffering or caching of images needed to control jittering and improve viewing and listening quality. Thus, there is clearly something to the proposed performance solution of the proprietary WAN common carriers.

This becomes an interesting solution if the proprietary network common carriers can offer services at costs comparable to the costs of using an Internet-based extranet today. So far they have not been able to do so, but the price difference between using the Internet and proprietary network services may narrow in the future. TCP/IP is likely to continue to be a preferred network standard because of the large number of vendors willing to support and maintain it.

The Fast Server Solution to the Audio/Visual Collaborative Computing

Whiteboard sharing of data is here today and represents an early collaborative computing solution over the extranet. However, video on demand

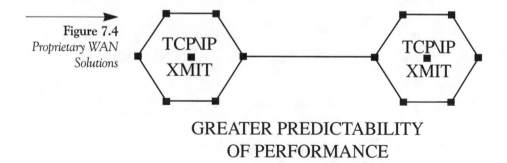

Figure 7.4
Proprietary WAN Solutions

and collaborative computing multimedia applications push the performance envelope of the Internet or extranet. Collaboration requires communication and a common set of tools and platforms used by all members of the collaborative teams!

Collaboration also requires recording the agreements that were made between members of the team. Usually, equal amounts of bandwidth and functionality and therefore of performance are not available to all members of the collaborative team because of the differences in the technical environments of team members. Adoption of standards and integration of computing platforms are elements of the solution to this problem.

For collaboration to occur, servers need to store large amounts of collaborative data and to simultaneously fill the collaborative connections of users to the server. This requires very fast servers and clusters of multiple processors sharing common memory and that use a network backbone or very fast high bandwidth bus for communication between the processors. Today about ten video streams per disk are possible given disk seeking constraints and switching constraints. This is a good rule of thumb for the constraints on audio/visual collaborative computing from current disk technology.

The fast server solution is often referred to as the "collapsed backbone" or "metacomputer." The idea of a metacomputer is that the network and the resources attached to it behave as one very fast computer because the network operates at the bus transfer speeds normally found in the back plane of a single computer. The metacomputer idea has been implemented over 100 megabit networks and does in fact work well for applications that are designed to be worked on in parallel by more than one computer.

The metacomputer idea represents one type of "end to end solution" or way around the classical performance problems of store and forward and/or routing designs (see Figure 7.5).

Figure 7.5
The Fast Server or Metacomputer Solution

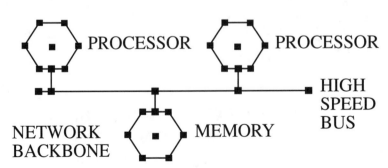

Fast servers need to quickly set up and tear down connections to other servers and clients in order to improve the performance of the extranet. This is because during much web-based communication more time is spent setting up and tearing down connections than is spent actually transferring files. Thus, switching technology that can quickly establish point to point or point to multipoint connections is a key part of the performance solution. It's not unusual for 50–60 TCP/IP point to point connections per second that last on average 2.5 seconds to be established over the extranet. This is substantially higher than the 5–6 connections per second that lasted for minutes that was common in pre-web-based technologies.

A Gateway Solution to Performance Problems of the Extranet

Gateway computers that translate from one communication protocol to another say SNA to TCP/IP can also be used to improve the overall performance of an extranet that needs to access host computers for data and applications (see Note 7.4).

NOTE 7.4 ———————————▶

Gateway solution advantages:	Lets the mainframe run the optimum protocol
Offloads from the mainframe:	Protocol translation memory required Processing required

---

The three reasons for this are:

▶ The gateway can offload protocol translation processing from the mainframe.

▶ The gateway can offload the memory required for storing and translating protocol translation software and data.

▶ Perhaps, most importantly, all mainframes are usually optimized to run a native protocol, whatever it may be (i.e., SNA, etc.). They usually run this protocol much more efficiently than they run protocol translation software.

See Figure 7.6.

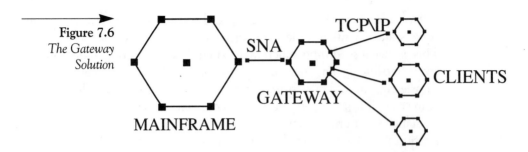

Figure 7.6
The Gateway
Solution

Of course communication protocol translation software could be placed on each and every client system, but the best network performance is usually achieved by placing the protocol translation software on gateway computers between multiple clients and the mainframe system. Today gateway machines and software support long lists of printers, terminals, PCs, and other network devices. The list varies with each gateway vendor.

In addition, gateway computers now perform many functions in addition to translating between different communication protocols including access control to the mainframe, security management, and network management, etc.

It is true that placing a gateway machine between clients and mainframe does add a small amount of processing overhead. However, this is more than made up for by the processing overhead removed from the mainframe. Performance can often be improved by scaling or increasing the number of gateway computers in front of the mainframe both horizontally and vertically.

Today gateway computers are often inexpensive Intel boxes that not only do protocol translation but many other things as well including controlling access to the mainframe, authenticating users, managing security, and performing network management functions. Some gateways can manage servers and other networked devices remotely and from either the mainframe or local area network side of the gateway. This is important because the network manager does not want to visit every desktop in person in order to reconfigure and manage desktop devices. Some gateways support as many as 2,000 users. Their consolidation requires traffic analysis and challenges remote server and network management.

However, server consolidation and the integration of network management tools into a windows environment decreases the amount of training and learning needed by the staff to manage remote networks. The features and benefits as well as reliability offered by gateway machines is likely to grow with time.

The reliability issue is often addressed today by running two gateway machines, one of which functions as a hot back up for the other. The gateways are not clustered in the sense that they do not share disks and other resources, but cut over to the other is automatic if the first should fail for any reason. If cut over occurs, users experience very brief disruption to their session or the quick starting of a new session on the mainframe.

A Best Performance Investment

According to the article "Your Best Performance Investment" (Van Name and Catchings, March 1998), the best investment you can make is the right set of performance monitoring procedures and tools.

Today many web servers provide static pages only to browsers. Performance can be increased by caching these pages in the web servers RAM memory and not on the server's hard drive. For maximum performance, only 5–10% of pages requested should come from the web server's disk. Both NT PerfMon and Netscape Enterprise Server 3.0 will report these statistics.

Most operating systems include tools to measure processor utilization. When web server processor utilization exceeds 90%, the processor usually does not have enough time to both run the web server application and to manage cache memory, so performance suffers.

Likewise, the network subsystem use should not exceed 80% or performance is likely to degrade. Network General's Sniffer is one product that can keep track of network utilization rates for you.

Also your business plan needs to dictate whether or not your greatest concern is average performance or performance under peak load. If your greatest concern is average performance, then you should monitor under conditions of average performance and be willing to offer lower performance at peak load times of the day. If your greatest concern is performance under peak load, then you should monitor under peak load and offer lower performance at other times of the day.

There are several industrial extranets that manage to achieve consistently high levels of extranet performance. For example, ADT Automotive Inc. is one of the top three wholesale vehicle distributors in the nation and was the first in its industry to implement on-line real-time interactive auctioning over the Internet. On-line banking and financial services have to offer consistent high performance because of the general consumers unwillingness to wait long for service. Bank Austria offers on-line banking services to 80,000 customers over its highly available, reliable, and secure extranet.

Chapter Summary

The performance solutions discussed in this chapter include:

▶ Understanding the relationship between usage and performance.

▶ Avoidance of store and forward systems and routing systems in favor of end to end systems for moving audio/visual files across the extranet especially in real time.

▶ Use of compression standards like JPEG and MPEG.

▶ Reliance on systems that can retrieve files in the background while the user runs some other applications in the foreground.

▶ Reliance on annotation and other collaboration tools that minimize the sending of entire files back and forth across the network.

▶ A proposed solution from providers of proprietary WAN-based network services for the performance predictability and quality predictability problems of the extranet.

▶ The fast server solution to the audio/visual collaborative computing performance problem.

▶ The gateway solution to the performance problems of the extranet.

▶ A best performance investment.

Cameras, speakers, microphones, a computer, software, and an Internet connection were mentioned as some of the elements required to send and receive audio/visual files over an extranet. By way of a final summary for this chapter, here is a table that combines the performance problems discussed in this chapter with their solutions. I believe that these solutions greatly enhance the ability of extranets to transmit real-time audio/visual data and therefore promote the use of extranets for applications like real-time auctions and commerce over the extranet.

Table 7.2 *Performance Problems and Solutions for Extranets*

Problem	Solution Discussed in This Chapter
Delay due to non-business use of the extranet	Understand user statistics and make extranet deployment decisions appropriately
Delay due to store and forward and routing systems	End to end systems or desktop to desktop systems Tools that work around store and forward and routing delays
Truncation or dropping of large files crossing the extranet	File compression algorithms and standards like wavelet, fractal, JPEG, and MPEG
System lock up while retrieving large files	Systems that can retrieve files in the background while the user runs applications in the foreground
Limited network bandwidth available for collaboration	Annotation and editing tools that can send just the changes to files back and forth across the network
Network performance and quality predictability problems	Running your extranet across a proprietary WAN
Filing the pipes or connections for extranet collaboration	The fast extranet server solution
Offloading the mainframe or host machines to improve network performance	The gateway machine and software solution

8

Managing Extranets

Chapter Objectives

This chapter examines the challenges of managing extranets and discuss the solutions that extranet implementers are using today to overcome the challenges of managing their extranets. In particular, this chapter discusses:

▶ A definition of the words "extranet management" and a comparison of the meaning of the words "extranet management" to the meaning of the words "extranet administration."

▶ Staffing ratios and requirements for extranet management.

▶ The need for an extranet inventory and an extranet database to store the results of the extranet inventory.

▶ Challenges and solutions to the problems of remote software upgrades and remote system management.

▶ Resolution of domain names into TCP/IP addresses to accomplish load balancing and redundancy.

▶ Use of tools to accomplish extranet management. This discussion examines the functionality needed by extranet managers rather than the details of any particular tool. Thus, the discussion focuses on ping, trace route, whois, etc.

▶ Continuous monitoring of extranets including use and parsing of log files, triggers, alarms, and trouble tickets.

▶ Fault tolerant and disaster recovery scenarios and solutions including backup and restore capabilities.

▶ Extranet management sizing.

After reading this chapter, you should have a good understanding of the functionalities and capabilities needed to successfully manage extranets. In addition, you should be better able to develop management solutions and to evaluate management tools for use with your extranet and in your environment.

According to figures presented at the Windows NT/Internet conference in San Francisco in the summer of 1997, Fortune 1000 firms lose on average $70,000 per hour when their corporate network is down. For enterprises conducting a high volume of business transactions over an extranet, the losses from extranet downtime could be much higher. The information presented in this chapter can help you make it less likely that your enterprise will suffer such losses from extranet downtime.

Definition of Extranet Management

Extranet management is a subset of the broader challenge of network and systems management. Thus, it deals with issues of accounting for use of an extranet, security, network or system faults, alarming, and trouble ticketing. Some of these issues are covered elsewhere in this book so they will not all be covered in this chapter.

Extranet administration is a subset of the broader challenge of network and systems administration that will be covered in the next chapter. Extranet administration deals with sharing or allocating extranet costs, designing and managing domains, adding and deleting users and accounts from an extranet, and dealing with changes to and growth of the extranet through policies and procedures.

Thus, extranet administration deals more with end users and business managers than with technology. On the other hand, extranet management deals more with technology than with end users and business managers in an effort to ensure that the extranet is available and fully functional whenever it is needed.

Staffing Ratios and Requirements for Extranet Management

Extranet managers just like their network management colleagues tend to be busy, overworked, and harassed people. Industry statistics vary, but in many companies there is one extranet or network manager for every 150 to 300 end users. Thus a ratio of 1/150 to 1/300 is a number commonly heard by this author at industry conferences and in case studies of network, intranet, and extranet management.

It is likely that the workload of extranet managers will increase in the future as extranet managers play a greater role in managing the security of their extranets. As explained in the chapter on security, extranet security is not guaranteed by encryption or authentication procedures alone. Threat analysis, parsing, scanning analysis of log files, and statistical analysis of usage and user profiles are also required to keep an extranet secure. These duties are ongoing and are likely to become more and more a part of the extranet manager's job.

The challenge of preventing router attacks illustrates this point nicely. Routers are computers dedicated to the job of moving messages or packets of data across a network.

It is usually the job of the network or extranet manager to manage router tables and to set the cost factors in these tables for transferring a message from router to router. Unfortunately, there is no authentication and access control between routers. Therefore, a router will accept any message commanding it to adjust the cost factors of its routing tables. If the cost factors are set very high, this will shut down the extranet because the router will not be able to identify a low-cost node or router to send messages to next.

The best way to detect and prevent router attacks is through scanning and statistical analysis of extranet usage. In fact, this is the only way to detect a truly sophisticated cracker who will enter the network with valid account names and passwords. Moreover, scanning and statistical analysis will be required to develop enough evidence to prosecute the sophisticated hacker. Some computer and network security experts estimate that there are only 220 law enforcement personnel in the entire United States dedicated to the investigation and prosecution of computer-based crimes. These people will not have time to statistically analyze usage of an extranet and gather evidence from usage profiles.

Instead, the gathering and documentation of such evidence is likely to become the responsibility of an extranet manager. If an extranet manager does not have time to gather and develop such evidence prosecution may be impossible. This fact, along with the fact that many organizations are very reluctant to publicly admit that their networks have been compromised, may explain why even very experienced network security experts are only able to see 50%–60% of cracker cases through to prosecution.

It is also worth noting that according to FBI statistics about 70% of all network break-ins come from those inside the organization. About 15% of that figure comes from break-ins over dial-up lines. Thus, network and extranet managers have to worry not only about threats from external sources but also from sources within the organization itself.

Certainly use of automated tools and smarter firewalls on every desktop can help ease the burden of extranet managers. However, sometimes managing the management tools themselves becomes a network management challenge especially if management of different tools is not well integrated or not an exercise in which one tool manages many devices.

Moreover, some network management tools shift work from network and extranet managers to end users. While this may decrease the number of network and extranet management staff that a firm needs to hire and thus lower network and extranet management costs, it does not lower total cost for the firm as a whole. This shifting of work to end users may, in fact raise, total cost and lower productivity to the firm as a whole. This is because shifting extranet management tasks to end users frequently lowers their overall productivity, distracts them from their primary job function, and forces them to take on a new learning curve in network and extranet management, a subject area that many of them have no interest in.

The implications of this for firms and managers considering the hiring of network and extranet management staff and the purchase of network and extranet management tools are clear. The objective of hiring more network and extranet management staff should be to lessen the burdens of and to increase the productivity of end users by making sure that the extranet is fully available, secure, and functional whenever and wherever it is needed. The objective of purchasing network and extranet management tools should be to lessen the burdens of network and extranet managers without shifting more work to end users; thus lowering total cost to the firm while increasing total productivity at the same time.

Therefore, from the perspective of the firm or enterprise as a whole, increases in total productivity and decreases in total cost are worthy objectives. Cost and productivity shifting are not desirable.

Need for Extranet Inventory and a Database to Store Results

Naturally, it is difficult to manage something when you have no knowledge of what it is that you are trying to manage. Unfortunately, many network and extranet managers find themselves in this position each and every day. Moreover, in many shops, the situation is actually worse than this because the network or extranet manager thinks that he or she knows what they are managing when they don't! Thus, it is not unusual to ask different people in an enterprise how many machines are on their extranet or even on their intranet and to receive widely varying answers. The head of Management Information Systems might believe that there are 3,000 machines on the network. The head of Network Management might believe that there are 5,000 machines on the network, and the head of Finance might believe that there are 1,000 machines on the network.

This happens because of the rapid growth and chaotic nature of many networks. For example, the Internet, intranets, and extranets are exploding in growth faster than anyone can imagine or keep up with. By some estimates, the dollar value of business transactions occurring over the Internet (including those occurring over extranets) will increase from about $8 billion in late 1996 to about $320 billion in 2002 or by a factor of about forty times according to figures presented at the 1997 NT/Internet Conference in San Francisco, California. In addition to the growth in the numbers of end users and business devices on the Internet, intranets, and extranets, there is rapid change occurring in the identity of end users and functionality of the devices on these networks. It should not be a surprise that managers have trouble tracking and keeping up with all of this growth and change.

Thus, frequently updated network inventories are the only way to begin to develop an accurate picture of extranets and intranets. This means that not only must a complete network inventory be taken but that the information that results from the inventory must be stored, available when needed, and easily updated. For this reason, some type of network inventory database is required for successful intranet or extranet management to occur. Fortunately, the tools available to accomplish this are growing in sophistication, power, and ease of use.

Challenges and Solutions to Remote Software Upgrades and Systems Management

Some of the challenges and problems of remote software upgrades and systems management illustrate the need for network inventories and a database to store the results of the network inventory. For example, in order to upgrade all of your desktop machines to the next version of an e-mail system you might need to know which machines have at least eight megabytes of random access memory along with 32 megabytes of available memory on their hard drive because machines that do not meet these requirements will not be able to run the new software in a satisfactory manner. If your enterprise has thousands of desktop machines acquired at different times or from different vendors, the only way to know this information is from a complete inventory of what is on the network along with a way to easily and quickly access the inventory information.

Of course, tools can help ease the burden of doing network and system inventories and thereby ease the burden of doing remote system upgrades and management. SMS from Microsoft is one such tool that grows more powerful with each release.

The consequences of upgrading desktop and other computers without any sort of inventory are greater expense and a longer time to complete the upgrades. This is especially true if a human being has to visit and touch every desktop in order to understand what's there and thereafter to upgrade or change what's there on the desktop. Use of automated network inventory tools and of good database technology to store and access network inventory information can help reduce the cost of upgrades and changes to the machines and devices on intranets and extranets.

Often, software upgrades of remote machines on the other side of an extranet do not work out as well as expected and there is need to analyze, redo, and undo the exercise or to recognize the problem, try again, and eventually fall back to the older software if the upgrade fails to be successful. Thus, the ability to fall back to older versions of the software following analysis and redo attempts is an important capability or functionality for distribution of software to remote machines on an extranet or intranet.

The capability of falling back to previous versions of software following analysis and redo attempts needs to be supported by primary and secondary domain back-up controllers.

Although back-up strategies are discussed later in this chapter, it is important to note here that a second back-up controller can greatly improve the reliability and dependability of extranet management. One back-up controller per domain is insufficient because if it fails and remains off line for long it will be impossible to fall back to earlier versions of software or other file types within that domain. (Estimates vary, but for NT some experts recommend 1,000 to 2,000 users per back-up controller in a single domain.)

One example of emerging technology that should help make extranet management and remote software upgrades and system management easier in the future is the development of directory services and directory-enabled applications. Gartner has estimated that the average Fortune 1000 firm has 181 separate directories in use for a wide variety of different purposes. Some of the directories look like telephone and address books of employee names. Other directories are used to locate departments, products, and prices, etc. Today, very few of these directories are used in any sort of integrated fashion. Updating, synchronizing, and replicating all of these directories across an enterprise network is a major technical challenge.

However, protocol standards are emerging that will help solve the directory access and integration problem for applications and network managers. Thus *LDAP* or Lightweight Directory Access Protocol is a simple directory access protocol with only about six functions that many vendors are adopting for use in better integrating applications to directories. This is important because directories can be viewed as single points of access to many applications, single points of administration, and as a way of lowering the total cost of network and system management and ownership. The basic idea is that an intranet or extranet manager should be able to manage a network by setting permissions and by performing software upgrades and remote system management at the directory level. The vision is that a network manager could upgrade software on remote systems by dragging and dropping an icon representing the new software to the top of a directory tree and every device that is part of the directory tree would be automatically upgraded to the new software. This technology has a ways to go yet before it can easily accomplish this goal, but it is likely to have very significant implications for intranet and extranet management.

Resolution of Names to TCP/IP Server Addresses for Load Balancing and Redundancy

Knowledgeable network and extranet managers can set up their TCP/IP domain name servers in ways that support load balancing and redundancy and thereby improve the reliability and performance of their networks. Extranet managers can do this by programming their domain name server to resolve the even numbered attempts to a connect to a server with a particular name to TCP/IP address . . . 1 and the odd numbered attempts to connect to a server with the same name to TCP/IP address . . . 2. Thus, queries to a server with a particular name are, in reality, spread across two servers. See the earlier discussion of round robin domain name/address resolution in Chapter 5. This kind of load balancing does require the existence of two identical or shadow servers. However, network performance improves because of the spreading of the load across multiple servers, and the network or system becomes more reliable because even if one of the servers is down one half of the queries will get through to the other server.

There are many variations on this scheme for increasing the reliability and performance of extranets via network management of domain name servers, and the effective management of domain name servers is an important part of network and domain management. See Chapter 5 for a more detailed discussion of load balancing and redundancy via domain name server round robin and other techniques.

Use of Tools to Manage Extranets

A great deal can be said about individual and particular tools for managing extranets. However, the goal here is not to give a feature by feature comparison of particular extranet management tools but instead to describe some of the logic of using tools to manage extranets and to point out some of the critical functionality required for effective management of extranets with tools.

The logic of tool use for managing extranets is much like the logic of using tools to manage wide area networks. Thus, it is important to analyze or diagnose problems, to verify understanding of problems by recreating them, and to undo problems by falling back to earlier versions of hardware, software, configurations, and settings. There are several functionalities that can help extranet managers apply this logic of extranet management.

Thus, there are tools that trace the path of a packet of information through routers and network hops and report this information back to the network manager so that the network or extranet manager can identify the sources of or extranet nodes causing congestion or loss of information.

Likewise, there are tools that will send a packet of information to a remote computer or ping a remote computer and listen for an acknowledgment. An extranet manager can use this information to determine whether or not a remote computer is, in fact, reachable over the network. Another set of tools will resolve names into TCP/IP addresses so that an extranet manager can discover exactly what devices and/or desktops are connected to an extranet at any point in time.

A whois database of names, addresses, and telephone numbers of end users and other network managers is often an extremely useful tool for an extranet manager especially when an extranet crosses several domains and there is more than one network manager involved in managing an extranet. Browsers themselves can function as extranet management tools. For example, Hewlett-Packard's Web JetAdmin lets network managers install, configure, and monitor different types of printers with Netscape's Navigator or Microsoft's Internet Explorer browser.

There is an HP Web tool that uses Java applets to manage any Management Information Base printers and to allow updates of device status changes. In addition, the product includes an automated mapping system that gives network managers a virtual office map or layout allowing them to plan for the optimum distribution of printer resources.

The goal of future versions of this product and others like it from other vendors will be to provision a single system that will locate, diagnose, and manage all peripheral devices installed on a network from a browser. These are just some of the basic or minimal functionalities and capabilities required to manage extranets.

Monitoring Extranets Including Log Files, Triggers, Alarms, and Trouble Tickets

Effective management of extranets requires continuous monitoring of extranets and especially of log files. Developing usage profiles and looking for anomalies in those usage profiles is key to successful extranet management.

Statistical analysis of the data in usage log files can be used to set triggers for alarms that can be used to alert extranet management staff when things go wrong. A trouble ticket or description of the problem along with an associated work order can be automatically issued to extranet management staff to isolate and fix the problem.

Unfortunately, many organizations ignore their activity or usage logs until after a network or security problem has occurred. This means that not only were problems not avoided or prevented in the first place but in addition that gigabytes of log files were allowed to accumulate on disks and now have to be examined when a problem occurs. The examination of all of that data can take lots of time.

A better methodology is for network or extranet managers to periodically, frequently, and regularly examine the log files in search of problems or breaches of security. This will result in less storage being needed for log files and in earlier recognition and resolution of extranet problems.

Fault Tolerance and Disaster Recovery Scenarios and Solutions

Fault tolerance usually refers to instantaneous or nearly immediate recovery from a network or system failure. The idea is that recovery is so quick and smooth that end users don't perceive the failure or at least don't perceive any damage from the failure. *Disaster recovery* on the other hand refers to recovery from a network or system fault or failure in some planned period of time that could be from minutes to weeks in duration.

The important thing to understand about these two terms is that they both imply the existence of a "time to recovery/cost ratio." In other words, the shorter the time to recovery desired the more money that must be spent to achieve that shorter time to recovery. The longer the allowed time to recovery, the less the amount of money that must be spent to achieve that time to recovery.

Back-up of software and data files is the key to successful disaster recovery. *Full back-up* means just what it says. It refers to copying everything to magnetic tape or other media and storing the magnetic tape or other media off line in a secure facility. *Differential back-up* refers to copying and storing only those files that have changed since the last back-up. *Incremental back-up* refers to copying to magnetic tape and storing files according to regular time increments. Files can be copied or copied along with having an archive bit set to restrict access types so that the copied files cannot be changed later.

Often companies will use combinations of all of these back-up strategies to save on magnetic tape while protecting or securing as many files as possible. Usually, a critical part of back-up strategy is to build and archive a catalog of what is on which magnetic tapes so that files can be easily found and recovered long after they are backed up and copied to magnetic tapes.

Random arrays of inexpensive disks or RAID can be used to increase system performance as well as to support fault tolerance and/or disaster recovery. The important principle to understand about RAID is the number of disks per disk controller. Thus, sometimes one disk controller is used to strip or write data across several different disks. Although this does not contribute to fault tolerance or disaster recovery, it does increase system performance by decreasing the amount of time that the computer spends seeking or looking for information on a disk. On the other hand, sometimes two controllers support multiple disks (disk smearing). This does enhance disaster recovery and fault tolerance because one controller can take over when the other fails.

An important part of fault tolerance and disaster recovery is *fail over* or switching to a hot or running back-up machine when a disaster or fault occurs. *Fail back* refers to going back to an older machine or version of the software to achieve fault tolerance or disaster recovery. *Active, active* mode refers to running two machines either of which can fail over to the other. *Active, passive* mode refers to running a hot back-up machine that is performing some secondary function until the primary machine fails at which point the hot back-up machine suspends its former task and takes over the primary task from the primary machine.

In some instances the computers involved in fault tolerance or disaster recovery schemes do not share data and programs; instead they perform separate tasks. However, if one machine fails for any reason, the other machines in the group are capable of taking over the functions of the failed machine. This type of arrangement is often referred to as a *shared nothing* configuration because the machines involved do not share data or programs. In order for another machine to take over from a failed machine, it must first be loaded with software and data from back-up media.

In contrast to a shared nothing configuration, there is a *shared everything* configuration in which all machines in the group share software and data. When one machine fails for any reason, another machine in the group can take over the function of the failed machine very quickly because it is already preloaded with software and data.

Fault tolerance and disaster recovery are likely to be critical issues for implementers of extranets and especially for those enterprises running a high volume of business transactions over their extranet. The average losses of $70,000 per hour for Fortune 1000 firms that experience network downtime that were mentioned earlier in this chapter may seem like pocket change to a firm that can no longer accept orders over its extranet or process stock transactions over its extranet. Fortunately, some of the fault tolerant and disaster recovery techniques mentioned above can help minimize some of the potential damage from network downtime.

Extranet Management Sizing

Here is some rough sizing data based upon the author's experience working on several extranets. This information is meant to be food for thought rather than a precise answer on sizing.

An extranet of 400 distributed servers, 40,000 users, 40,000 web pages, and a constantly changing number of links was managed by a technical staff of about 130, half of which were contractors and half of which were full-time employees. About a half dozen content providers worked on this particular extranet which was up 24 hours a day and 365 days a year.

Chapter Summary

This chapter has taken a close look at:

▶ A definition of the words "extranet management" and a comparison of the meaning of the words "extranet management" to the meaning of the words "extranet administration."

▶ Staffing ratios and requirements for extranet management.

▶ The need for an extranet inventory and an extranet database to store the results of the extranet inventory.

▶ Challenges and solutions to the problems of remote software upgrades and remote system management.

▶ Resolution of domain names into TCP/IP addresses to accomplish load balancing and redundancy.

▶ Use of tools to accomplish extranet management. This discussion examines the functionality needed by extranet managers rather than on the details of any particular tool. Thus, the discussion focuses on ping, trace route, whois, etc.

▶ Continuous monitoring of extranets including use and parsing of log files, triggers, alarms, and trouble tickets.

▶ Fault tolerant and disaster recovery scenarios and solutions including backup and restore capabilities.

▶ Extranet management sizing.

Extranet management is likely to be one of the more exciting areas of extranet research and development in the future because of the strong market need and demand for integrated tools to better manage and secure extranets. These tools are likely to grow out of the existing suite of wide area network, intranet, and Internet management tools and to be used by enterprises and individuals to manage their WANs. Next we look at extranet administration as opposed to extranet management.

9

Administering Extranets

The discussion in this chapter focuses on extranet administration or:

▶ Extranet cost savings

▶ Domain designs

▶ Adding and deleting user accounts

▶ Setting permissions and privileges

▶ Accounting for and sharing extranet costs

▶ Policies and procedures and business process steps

▶ Help desk support

As you can see from this list, the focus is more on end users and managers than on technology. Extranet management challenges, solutions, and technologies were discussed in the previous chapter.

Extranet Cost Savings

One of the key reasons for the popularity of extranet technology is the wide area network cost savings that some enterprises are able to realize from implementing extranet technology. These savings are especially likely to be realizable when extranets cross geographic boundaries or span long distances and the same or compatible Internet Service Providers can be found at both ends of the extranet.

For example, one of the speakers at the Windows NT/Intranet trade show in the late summer of 1997 claimed that by dropping Integrated Services Digital Network connections in favor of extranet connections implemented via Internet Service Providers, he was able to lower wide area networking line costs from $35,000 per month to $10,000 per month for his clients. Indeed, there seems to be something of a price war going on between long hall WAN providers and Internet Service Providers with wide area line costs dropping as low as $7,000 per month according to some of the presenters at the Windows NT/Internet trade show.

Cost savings like these are likely to please any wide area network administrator or high-level manager. However, it should be noted that these cost savings are only achievable where Internet Service Providers are well established and willing to offer competitive rates. Although this is true in much of the United States today, this is clearly not the case in every country or locality of the world today. Although in many cases individuals in the United States can obtain Internet access for up to about eighteen hours per month for a flat fee of about $10 (exclusive of the cost of the telephone call to the Internet Service Provider), there are parts of Africa and Asia where reliable Internet access is either very expensive or not available at all.

The achievement of significant cost savings is likely to be a key goal of most extranet administrators. A good understanding of Internet Service Provider rates and billing practices will be needed to accomplish this goal. Thus, extranet administrators need to know that Internet Service Providers usually charge either a flat monthly rate for unlimited Internet access or a per hour charge for Internet access. In some cases, a blended rate is offered. A blended Internet access rate is a billing scheme by which the Internet Service Provider charges a flat fee for so many hours of Internet access per month up to some maximum amount and a per hour rate for Internet access above and beyond the maximum amount of monthly Internet access allowed.

Extranet administrators also need to know that nomadic and traveling employees are likely to run up higher Internet (and therefore extranet access charges). These employees will either place long distance calls to Internet Service Providers or will be using 800 telephone numbers provided by Internet Service Providers who usually charge more when they offer 800 telephone number services.

Extranet administrators will find extranet usage statistics extremely useful when it comes to negotiating with Internet Service Providers and assessing proposals for wide area network connection costs. Thus, usage statistics need to be regularly accumulated and reviewed.

Domain Designs

Domain designs and architecture can make the job of extranet administration either much easier or much harder. This is because domains are basically groups of servers, clients, and devices that trust each other and are willing to share resources with each other. In other words, a domain or subdomain is a unit of trust, resource sharing, management, and administration. Within a domain, trust relationships make the setting of user permissions and privileges easier and subdomains often inherit their permissions and privilege settings from a parent domain.

Often the best domain designs and architectures reflect organizational structures or geography. In the case of organizations that change and reorganize frequently, geographical structuring of domains is often preferred to organizational structuring of domains. This is because the redesign or architecting of domains results in substantial disruption to networks and inconvenience to end users. Thus, network managers and administrators try to avoid it whenever possible.

The default domain design is often to declare everything one giant domain. This makes little or no sense in the case of extranets where geography and distance do matter. It is more logical to design extranet domains in terms of geographic units. Thus, a distant branch office or division might represent one domain with several subdomains. In other words, extranet administrators and managers require a domain architecture that breaks their job of administering and managing a network up into a hierarchy of logical units so that the domain and subdomain structures make administration and management of an extranet easier.

Adding and Deleting User Accounts and Setting Permissions and Privileges

Intranets and extranets tend to grow and change extremely rapidly. This makes the job of administering them extremely challenging. One solution is to divide and conquer by dividing the network into domains and subdomains and giving each domain and/or subdomain its own extranet administrator and manager.

This works fine in terms of adding and deleting end user accounts and in terms of setting end user permissions and privileges at the local level. Unfortunately, this solution encounters severe difficulties as soon as problems that span several domains or subdomains appear. A good example of this is the problem of replicating and synchronizing directories of information that span the entire enterprise. In this case, extranet administrators may spend more time fighting turf wars than they spend effectively administering the extranet.

Part of the solution to this problem is technical in that the emergence of better enterprise wide directory management software can make directory replication and synchronization less of an administrative night-mare. The same can be said in terms of administering the assignment and reassignment of TCP/IP addresses to device names or in terms of assigning and keeping track of end user passwords. Since many of the technology solutions to these problems have been discussed elsewhere in this book, they will not be discussed or repeated here.

However, part of the solution is also extranet policies and procedures that remove much of the ambiguity from the extranet administrator's job. Some of these policies and procedures need to offer solutions to the problem of fairly accounting for extranet usage and associated costs.

Accounting for and Sharing of Extranet Costs

Accounting for and sharing of extranet costs is going to depend heavily on what people use their extranet for. An extranet can be used for most of the things that individuals use the Internet for today. Thus, an extranet can be used for e-mail exchange, electronic bulletin board access, news group access, commerce, education, training, and much more.

But in addition to all of these things, an extranet can be used for commercial and financial transactions. These multiple uses raise the issue of usage fees and transaction fees.

A *usage fee* is just what it says. It is a fee for using a resource be it hardware, software, or human. A *transaction fee* is a fee for engaging in a transaction or exchange of goods or services for other goods or services including wealth. The answer to the question of which type of fee is better depends upon just what it is that implementers are trying to do with their extranets. Transaction fees are usually applied to commercial transactions and usage fees are usually applied to the rent or lease of hardware, software, and other resources.

Although there is a long history of charging end users or end user departments for usage fees for using computer networks, there is a much shorter history of charging end users or consumers for electronic transactions implemented over a computer network. In fact, until very recently much of the technology necessary for charging for and implementing commercial transactions over extranets did not exist. This situation is changing rapidly as software developers come out with innovative products that make accounting for and billing commercial transactions over intranets, extranets, and the Internet much easier.

What makes these products unique is their ability to track and bill for exchanges of information over a computer network even for tiny amounts of information and for tiny amounts of money per transaction that add to large amounts of money when transactions are accumulated. Thus, some of these products can account for thousandths of a cent as just a few bytes or bits of information are exchanged. This is important because unless information providers can charge for their products and services the Internet, intranets, and extranets are unlikely to grow into true media for commercial transaction. The possibility of fairly accounting for and sharing of extranet costs is rapidly becoming a technical reality.

Policies and Procedures and Business Process Steps

Extranet policies and procedures should be driven by the business process steps that relate to your goal in implementing an extranet. Thus, if your goal is to sell stuff over an extranet, you need to understand your order processing and order management policies, procedures, and steps in detail and use those things to define and drive your extranet policies and procedures. If your goal is to publish a catalog over an extranet then you need to understand your catalog policies, procedures, and processes in detail and use those things to define and drive your extranet policies and procedures.

There are, of course, some policy and procedure questions that are unique to the Internet, intranets, and extranets. For example, some employers and governments are concerned that employees and others will use computer networks for illegal or immoral purposes.

Software developers have responded to these concerns by offering a variety of software products to block and filter material from specified web sites and to generate activity reports summarizing who has visited which web sites and how often. These products are supposed to make the job of the parent or extranet administrator attempting to police the network easier.

However, policing computer networks is not easy and technically creative people both young and old can generally find a way around the blocking and filtering programs. In addition, the implementation of these programs can be interpreted as a sign of lack of trust and can harm the relationship between parent and child or in the case of extranets between employer and employee.

Some organizations deal with this problem by explicitly establishing a contract between employee and employer or between student and school as to what is acceptable network behavior. This is often more effective than blockers, filters, and activity reports because it raises everyone's awareness of what is good network behavior and builds commitment to that behavior.

In any case, this is one of the more complex issues that extranet administrators will have to deal with. In the case of common carriers, network administrators may choose not to attempt to control access to objectionable materials because to do so may result in their legal status changing from that of common carrier to editor which will increase their legal responsibility for controlling the information sent over their network. On the other hand, some countries force extranet and network administrators to attempt to control the type of information sent over their network.

In the case of extranets where users rely upon the accuracy, reliability, and general trustworthiness of information received over extranets, extranet administrators will need to work with content providers to meet these needs. These issues are likely to be far more important to the success and credibility of extranets than to the success and credibility of the Internet with its sort of *anything goes* and free wheeling tradition. This is especially true in the case of commercial transactions done over an extranet. Thus, extranet administrators and managers need to understand business process steps better than ever before.

Help Desk Support

Help desk support, especially for traveling, roaming, nomadic, or mobile extranet users, is likely to be a significant challenge for extranet administrators. Fortunately many but not all of the standard help desk support approaches can be used for extranet help desk support as well as for help desk support for other types of networks.

Help desks traditionally offer front line support to end users when they get stuck and don't know what to do next. Usually, their technology is not working so they need to contact the help desk via some alternate system of technology. For example, if a remote user cannot connect to an extranet by dialing in over a particular telephone line, then the remote user will need access to a second telephone line which he or she can use to communicate with the help desk in order to receive support. If more than one telephone line is not available then the end user will be unable to obtain help desk support.

To be effective, help desk support needs to be available wherever and whenever end users need it. In the case of traveling and nomadic employees this often means that help desk support must be available 24 hours a day and seven days a week. This is also likely to be the case for extranet end users who span multiple time zones and who are often located long distances apart.

Help desk support personnel perform many different job functions. For example, in the case of extranet help desks support personnel will need not only extranet technical expertise but also business process expertise. Increasingly, help desks are staffed by people with both technical and business expertise as well as training or teaching expertise.

In fact, so many different levels of expertise are required to run an effective help desk operation that problems reported to a help desk must be triaged to be resolved.

For example, a help desk query from an extranet user may be a personnel computer problem, a server problem, a network transmission problem, a password or account name problem, or a problem executing one or more of the steps of a business process. No one can be an expert in all of these areas so the help desk organization must implement a triage process in order to have any chance at all of dealing with and resolving end user queries.

In the case of an extranet, a typical help desk support process might include the following steps:

1. A remote extranet user calls the help desk to report a problem using or connecting to the extranet.

2. The remote extranet user is asked to classify or identify his or her problem as personal computer related, extranet related, server related, or business process related, etc., by entering a number into a touch-tone telephone.

3. A specialist in the problem area identified by the remote extranet user answers the telephone call, talks with the user, logs the name and cost center of the user, records the symptoms of the problem, proposes a diagnosis, and suggests a solution or work around if possible.

4. The remote extranet user attempts to implement the fix or work around while on the telephone with the help desk support specialist.

5. If the fix or work around solves the problem, the help desk support specialist logs this result and e-mail a summary of the problem and fix to the user.

6. If the fix or work around fails or further research is needed, the help desk support specialist will leave the problem status open until the problem is resolved.

There are several things worth noting about this help desk extranet support process. First, unlike many of the traditional help desk support for technology operations, this process includes a problem category for business process implementation. This recognizes the fact that most extranets are implemented to support some type of business process and end users can be expected to have questions and need guidance when it comes to executing business processes. Second, not all problems reported to the help desk have an immediate solution or work around. Further research and discussion with experts in other areas or with supplier experts may be necessary to resolve the problem. The last item in the help desk process recognizes this.

As the help desk receives requests for help it classifies them and assigns priorities to fixing or resolving them. Problems that threaten the business transactions of the enterprise are likely to receive the highest priority and the most immediate attention. Problems that only impact a small number of users are likely to receive lower priority and a less immediate response.

The business significance of what the extranet does for the organization is likely to determine the priority and the speed of the response to extranet problems reported to the help desk. If an extranet is used for order processing and receipt of payments then the help desk is likely to assign a high priority to any problem that shuts it down. On the other hand, if an extranet is used only for exchanging e-mail with those outside the organization then the help desk is likely to assign a lower priority to problems that threaten to shut the extranet down. However, an extranet is in some sense a high visibility network precisely because it is extremely visible to those outside the enterprise. Thus, most problems regarding it are likely to be high priority problems for the help desk.

Help desk support personnel depend heavily on the use of tools to monitor, troubleshoot, and fix network problems. Thus, help desk support personnel study network logs, server transaction logs, and run trace and ping programs to confirm the availability of network links to remote servers.

Help desk support is clearly a key success factor for successful implementation of extranets. This is because help desk support plays a large role in setting end user expectations, training and educating end users, and in maintaining or improving end user productivity.

However, help desk operations sometimes generate their own share of junk e-mail and overhead announcements of system downtime and maintenance schedules. Junk mail and administrivia should be avoided on an extranet just as on any other network.

Unfortunately, many extranet implementations fail to consider the huge impact on help desk support of launching a new extranet. Not only can calls to the help desk be expected to explode during the initial roll out of the new network, but the calls will be coming from business partners and customers who may be both impatient and not computer or network literate at the same time.

To effectively handle this situation, help desk support personnel will need to be both technically and business literate as well as skilled with handling people. This is a tall order indeed and can only be achieved if good people are hired in the first place and are well trained to run the help desk.

There is an inverse relationship between the amount of money and effort spent on help desk infrastructure and training and the frustration that can be expected in implementing a new extranet. In other words, the more money and effort that goes into preparing the help desk for the initial roll out of a new extranet the more quickly end user frustrations and problems can be resolved and the greater the probability that the new extranet will be successful. Skimping on investment in the help desk will lower end user productivity and increase the likelihood that end users will perceive the new extranet as a less than useful tool or way to meet their needs.

Extranet implementation is likely to generate whole new categories of questions for help desk support personnel to answer. For example, extranet users are likely to have far more questions on business process steps and less knowledge of how the organization works than are end users internal to the organization. In addition, extranet end users are probably unable to get help and support from their colleagues sitting next to them who may not be using the extranet at all. It is important to recognize this fact and plan for it because when dealing with intranets and other internal systems end users often turn to each other for help and thereby avoid telephone calls to the help desk for support.

It is also important to understand that as a new extranet is rolled out and end users gain experience using it, the types of questions received by the help desk will change and evolve. Thus, initially the help desk will receive many questions on client upgrades and questions of compatibility and interoperability with the new extranet. After the initial flurry of questions about connecting to and getting local equipment to communicate with the remote equipment over the extranet, there will be questions on process steps and how to use the full functionality of the extranet. Finally, there may be questions on or suggestions for improving the overall quality and usefulness of the extranet.

Extranet help desk support for small, medium, and large enterprises is similar because extranet help desk support is fundamentally support for wide area networks. The application level support for extranets is similar to the application level support needed for intranets and other networks internal to the enterprise.

In the very near future, the standard help desk query process will include a category for extranet problem resolution. This help desk support category will need to resolve questions of wide area network support and business processes in addition to dealing with end users in remote areas, in different times zones, and possibly speaking different languages.

The extranet itself is a tool that can be used to provide better help desk support. For example, consider the following table:

Table 9.1 *The Possible Role of an Extranet in the Help Desk Support Process*

Help Desk Support Process	Role of an Extranet
1. Record problems and resolutions	Facilitate this through wide area communications
2. Publish policies and procedures	Facilitate this through wide area communications
3. Publish security recommendations	Facilitate this through wide area communications
4. Deliver new software to remote sites	Facilitate this through wide area communications

As you can see from this table, there are many areas in which the wide area communication functionality of an extranet can be used to improve help desk support.

Chapter Summary

This chapter has focused on extranet administration including help desk support. The chapter discussed:

▶ Extranet cost savings

▶ Domain designs

▶ Adding and deleting user accounts

▶ Setting permissions and privileges

▶ Accounting for and sharing extranet costs

▶ Policies and procedures and business process steps

▶ Help desk support

In this chapter, *administration* was defined as being focused on the management of end user accounts and questions rather than on the management of machines and technology as was the focus of the previous chapter on *extranet management*.

10

Future Challenges and Directions of Extranets

Chapter Objectives

This chapter explores future challenges and directions of extranets. Since attempting to predict the future especially the future of technology is a very risky business, this chapter discusses those things that are mostly like to influence the future direction of extranets rather than trying to predict that future itself. Thus, this chapter discusses:

▶ How corporate, government, and academic research and development are likely to influence extranets.

▶ Technology drivers of extranet growth, i.e., infrastructure and enabling technologies.

▶ Economic drivers of extranet growth.

▶ What creates and makes a community of extranet users grow.

▶ The stages of growth of a community of extranet users.

▶ What extranet owners and sponsors can do to help create and grow a community of extranet users.

▶ Potential conflicts between extranet owners or sponsors and extranet users.

▶ Things that you can do now to prepare for the future.

Let's start by looking at the role of different segments of society in funding and supporting research and development. After all, these institutions played a major role in developing Internet technology, perhaps they will play a major role in the future direction of extranets as well.

The Role of Corporations, Government, and Academia

Corporations, Government, and Academia have played a significant role in research and development, especially in Internet research and development (see Note 10.1). They are likely to play a significant role in extranet research and development in the future. Although these institutions have played a significant role in supporting research and development that lead to the Internet, intranets, and extranets, their roles have differed substantially.

NOTE 10.1 ————————➤

    Different Sources and Types of R & D

    Academia   →   theory

    Government   →   standards

    Corporate   →   products and services

Thus, corporations traditionally take a short-term view of research and development by expecting that the research and development will generate revenue and profit in four years or less and in many cases much less. Government takes a more medium-term view of research and development by expecting the research and development to lead to commercial results, i.e., employment and tax revenues in 10 to 20 years. Higher academic institutions take the long-term view of research and development by expecting the research and development to generate significant commercial and practical results in a generation or so. However, academic institutions often expect research and development to generate "interesting" theoretical results in much less than a generation.

Moreover, these institutions are much better at supporting some kinds of research and development rather than others. Thus, corporations are not very good at getting their competitors to adopt the types of technical standards that make TCP/IP, Internets, intranets, and extranets possible because the adoption of standards often does, in fact, lower corporate profit margins. Government-sponsored research is often better at this because the government can develop new technical standards and give them away to everyone without violating responsibility to shareholders. Government in the form of the Advanced Projects Research Agency has been a leader in the field of Internet research and without the government-sponsored research done in the past there would be no Internet, intranets, or extranets today.

On the other hand, government is not good at bringing commercial strength products and services to market. This is, instead, the strength of corporations. Unfortunately, because of the need to balance the federal budget, government funding of basic research is expected to decline significantly over the next several years.

Academic institutions, at least in the United States, are very good at generating peer-reviewed research and largely because of this fact the United States leads the world in information technology and in biotechnology. In the case of biotechnology especially, government labs have complemented the advanced research work done in academia.

The implications of this for the future of extranets are fairly clear in that effective technology standards are most likely to result from government-sponsored research, great theoretical breakthroughs are most likely to come from academia, and great new products and services are most likely to come from corporations.

Extranets, intranets, and the Internet would all benefit from new tools to diagnose Internet traffic delays and path congestion. In the past, these tools came from government labs. In the future they should come from corporations. The transition from academic theory to government lab to commercial enterprise to commercial products and services is likely to be the normal path for extranet and other technologies.

Technology Drivers of Extranet Growth

Many forms of technology have helped to drive extranet growth. Infrastructure and enabling technologies have been and are likely to continue to be important technology drivers of extranet growth in the future (see Note 10.2).

NOTE 10.2 ────────▶

Next Generation Internet Projects

100	10
Universities connected 100 times faster	Universities connected 1000 times faster

- Better trace route and path care
- Better security and billing

Thus, there are next generation Internet, intranet, and extranet projects being talked about in government and academic circles to drive network infrastructure and enabling technologies forward. For example, there is a project (Internet2) to connect 100 universities with a network 100 times faster than the existing Internet backbone. There is also a project to connect 10 universities with a network 1000 times faster than the existing Internet backbone.

Faster Internet backbones and connections are the key to the emergence of a whole new class of exciting Internet, intranet, and extranet applications. For example, Internet TV is already being used in a few places in Silicon Valley where very fast network backbone connections are already available. Internet TV displays video images in semi-realtime of collaborators as they exchange messages via audio or e-mail. The images displayed are somewhat jerky and grainy but the technology is sure to get better with time. Internet telephone is similar to Internet TV but lacks the video information exchange and thus requires less bandwidth. Even so, Internet telephone does push Internet connections to their limits today.

There is an exciting conversation going today about the eventual merging of television and Internet technologies (see Note 10.3).

NOTE 10.3 ⟶

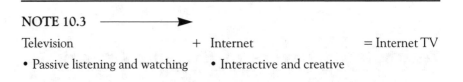

Television	+ Internet	= Internet TV
• Passive listening and watching	• Interactive and creative	

The debate is less about the technical feasibility of doing this in the future than about potential markets and consumer desires for such a merger of technologies. Some people argue that people watch TV when they want to sit passively and be entertained. These same people argue that consumers turn on their computers when they want to interact with their machines or other people and be creative. Thus, TV is described as passive entertainment and the Internet or computers are described as interactive and creative. At the present time, it's anyone's guess as to whether or not consumers really want to see a merger of these two technologies and would be willing to pay for the resulting new technology. However, the research and development is being done to combine Internet and television technologies and commercial experiments and test marketing are likely to follow.

It is interesting to note that although the Internet, intranets, and extranets require a technology infrastructure in order to operate effectively, some would argue that access to the Internet is now part of the basic infrastructure required for a sound education. Others point out that Internet access aids education only when parents, teachers, and children are all engaged in the educational process. In other words, the Internet is a wonderful tool but it is no substitute for a good or positive educational environment.

It is important to note that part of the infrastructure required for the successful operation of the Internet, intranets, and extranets are skilled or educated end users. End users who can't spell, understand basic grammar, or do elementary mathematics are not likely to benefit from the information available over any kind of network. Thus, education in basic reading, writing, and mathematics skills is one of the elements of basic infrastructure needed for successful use of the Internet, intranets, and extranets. Unfortunately, this key element of infrastructure is not readily available in all parts of the world or even of the United States today.

Yet another element of infrastructure or enabling technology for the Internet, intranets, and especially for extranets is security and encryption. Stronger encryption algorithms and attempts to break them are ongoing. The significant issues around security technologies are social and legal. So far, the United States government has resisted the widespread deployment of codes and encryption technologies that it cannot break. The government does not want to see its enemies armed with unbreakable codes and secret communications.

Some kind of compromise between those who want widespread deployment of this technology and the United States government may yet occur through the various key escrow proposals now before the government and industry. The widespread deployment of security technology is likely to have a huge impact on the growth or nongrowth of extranets. After all, few businesses are willing to share their information with anyone and everyone who might be listening to their extranet.

The ability to charge for small and large amounts of intellectual property and information delivered across extranets is also likely to drive the growth of extranets. After all, content providers are not likely to welcome extranets with open arms if they cannot charge for and be paid for their creations. If content providers don't flock to an extranet, users are not likely to come either. Thus, technologies that account for and can bill for intellectual property and information delivered across extranets are likely to significantly influence the long-term growth of extranets.

The widespread availability of network personal computers may also cause extranets to grow in the future by lowering both the upfront and ongoing costs of connecting to extranets. Network computers are thought by some people to be cheaper to purchase and less costly to maintain than personal computer. For those who don't want or need the power of a fully loaded personal computer, network personal computers are a good way to connect to extranets. The widespread availability of network personal computers may help lead to the widespread availability of extranets.

Economic Drivers of Extranet Growth

The two great economic drivers of extranet growth are, of course, the ability to use extranets to save money and or to generate revenue. Extranets can save firms money by lowering paper and postage costs and by increasing the productivity of geographically dispersed work teams. This is a natural extension of what organizations are doing with intranets and the Internet today.

The potential of an extranet to increase revenues is exciting, but unfortunately is seldom realized in practice today. There are many reasons for this failure of practice. For one thing, many firms don't monitor their extranet well or intranets and Internet connection. These organizations have no real way of knowing whether or not their extranet is contributing to the bottom line.

Even when firms do monitor their extranet web sites and regularly gather usage statistics, they often measure only hits or queries to their web sites. They have no idea how long users stay at their extranet web site or what the users are there for. Increased web site monitoring and analysis of statistics can significantly increase an organization's chances of making or saving money with its web sites.

What Creates and Makes a Community of Extranet End Users Grow?

This is likely to be a crucial question for designers and implementers of extranet web sites because without a community of dedicated end users to support it an extranet is almost sure to die (see Note 10.4). Indeed, many companies as well as individual producers of information will invest in extranets for the explicit purpose of expanding markets for their products and services via electronic and virtual communities.

NOTE 10.4 ————————▶

Internet and Extranet Growth Drivers

✓ Shared interests

✓ Relationships

✓ Transactions

People join electronic communities in order to satisfy certain basic needs, especially a need to connect with other people on an ongoing basis that fosters trust. Often, members of an electronic community share a passionate interest in something and wish to communicate with others who share that same interest. Those interests are enormously varied and define every kind of niche market available. Everything from martial arts to stamp collecting to investing has a home and group of interested people pursuing it on the world wide web.

Often the members of these electronic groups share not only a common interest but a great deal of expertise as well. Indeed, such groups thrive on information, knowledge, and debate in their particular narrow field of interest.

The emergence of independent electronic bulletin boards directly feeds this passion for a particular interest. These bulletin boards are usually operated by individual system operators who share a passion for the subject of the bulletin board. Often, electronic bulletin boards represent a grass roots movement and are not sponsored or funded by corporations or other large organizations. At one time, these electronic bulletin boards could only be reached by dialing a particular telephone number and connecting via a modem. However, this has changed rapidly and today most of the electronic bulletin boards are reachable via an Internet connection. The audience for these bulletin boards is incredibly diverse and represents every type of consumer and interest imaginable.

It is important to note that professional organizations have also exploited the electronic bulletin board concept with a significant amount of success. Thus, organizations like the American Bar Association, American Medical Association, and Software Support Professionals Association all have electronic bulletin boards.

Although many people are quick to join electronic communities that share their interests, they will not remain members of the electronic community for long unless they can form positive relationships with their on-line colleagues. Much of the power of virtual communities is that they enable people with similar experiences to communicate across time and distances. Common interests and experiences born of trauma are a good example of this. Thus there are on-line support groups for divorce, loss or death of loved ones, and people diagnosed with fatal or chronic diseases. Indeed, there are even on-line support groups for people with addictions to chemical substances.

Often the result of communicating with such groups for a new member of an electronic community is a set of powerful life-long relationships with others. Many times the communication begins with a request for information, but rapidly changes to an exchange of personal experiences that form the basis for deep relationships. The exchange of personal experiences or interactivity and production or documentation of personal experiences makes membership in a virtual community unique and powerful. Writing a letter to request information on cancer and receiving a brochure is a far less powerful than sharing personal experiences fighting the disease with others in a similar situation.

Many of these virtual communities represent natural target markets for various businesses. For example, SeniorNet maintains electronic forums targeted at senior citizens and which cover a wide range of topics of interest to senior citizens. Some of the topics covered are Christian Corner, Federal Retirees, and Divorced Pals. More and more retired people own and are flocking to computers and on-line services, creating new markets for an enormous range of products and services.

Not everyone joins an electronic community for serious reasons. Many people joining electronic communities are simply looking for entertainment and especially for interactive entertainment that involves the sharing of their fantasies with others. Games like Multi-User Dungeon abound in which users act out their fantasy roles with each other. Simulation games, war games, and games of business competition are also played out in electronic communities.

However, almost everyone who joins an electronic community engages in transactions in the sense of trading or exchanging information. The concept of trading in the sense of information exchange has been with the Internet since the earliest days of the net. In fact, electronic discussion groups often shun those who simply want to take information and never share it. Today the concept of trading information is rapidly expanding to include the exchange of wealth for products or services. This is creating yet more new markets for owners and sponsors of extranets.

Stages of Growth of a Virtual Community of Users

It is important that companies or organizations launching extranets understand why and how virtual communities expand and grow (see Note 10.5).

NOTE 10.5 ————————➤

Stages of Growth in Extranet Communities

✓ Critical mass of users

✓ Critical mass of user profiles

✓ Critical mass of ads

✓ Critical mass of transactions

In some sense, the successful growth of any virtual community whether supported by the Internet, intranets, or extranets is about the accumulation of critical mass, i.e., a critical mass of end users, a critical mass of content providers, a critical mass of transactions, a critical mass of usage profiles, a critical mass of advertisers, and a critical mass of end user loyalty.

Electronic communities are self-fulfilling prophecies in the sense that success breeds success and failure breeds failure more so than in many other areas of business and life.

This is because of all of the reasons that support the growth of electronic communities in the first place. The sharing of information and personal experiences in areas of common interest, the building of deep relationships, sharing of fantasies, and engaging in information and financial transactions all require a minimum mass of engaged users to be effective.

In the first stage of growth of an electronic community enough end users have to be attracted to break through the magic threshold that will eventually make the electronic community become self-sustaining and grow. This immediately gives rise to a chicken and egg growth problem. Great content is the best way to attract new end users to an electronic community and to keep them there. However, much of the content in any successful electronic community is created by the members of that community. The chicken and egg problem is that without content the electronic community can't attract new members and keep old ones, and without members the electronic community can't generate content. Attracting the critical mass of end users necessary to solve the chicken and egg problem is the first milestone in the growth of any successful electronic community.

The next milestone in the successful growth of an electronic community is the reaching of a critical mass of transactions that can support and grow the electronic community. The critical mass of transactions can be exchanges of information or dollars and products or services between end users. Without a critical mass of transactions the electronic community cannot financially or intellectually sustain itself. Achieving this critical mass of transactions is critical.

Usage and user profiles are the lifeblood of many electronic communities that exist to engage in commercial transaction. This is because these communities cannot attract vendors and advertisers without evidence that it will pay commercial organizations to sponsor or join the electronic community. Statistics on membership and the interests of members are usually what attracts commercial organizations to a virtual community in the first place.

The most successful on-line communities manage to generate an enormous degree of member loyalty. Loyalty is likely to be a key issue in the success of extranets as well as other types of virtual communities. The reason for this is that surfing the web is extremely expensive for the owner of the web site and doesn't generate much revenue either. Thus, there has been a change going on the way web site statistics are gathered. Today knowledgeable people ask how many end users "clicked through their web site" to actually request information or engage in a transaction rather than how many end users simply visited their web site. When "click throughs" are counted rather than "hits" or visits to web sites, many of the sites are much less successful than was initially perceived. Often a high number of hits does not go with a high number of click throughs.

Almost all of the on-line services struggle to maintain loyalty. As the available number of end users is gobbled up by on-line services and it becomes harder and harder to replace lost members, member loyalty grows in importance.

What Extranet Owners and Sponsors Can Do

Achieving a critical mass of end users to fuel the growth of an extranet or any other form of electronic community is a matter of speed and preemption. You need to generate, concentrate, and lock in the end users before someone else does.

The best way to accomplish this is to choose a niche, target market, or narrow field of interest as an initial focus for your extranet. However, the choice of a narrow field of interest needs to be capable of growing and broadening and attracting a wider and wider audience. For example, the initial focus of an extranet might be to offer people information on dentistry for young children. This topic could easily broaden to include information on dentistry for adults as well as young children. The initial topic of interest for an electronic community needs to be chosen with great care so as to balance investment or resources consumed and the risk that a critical mass of end users will never form.

The key to success is to focus on individual user needs and to keep expanding offerings over an extranet so as to concentrate and lock in traffic. Lurkers and surfers need to be engaged quickly and turned into ongoing members of an extranet community.

As an extranet community grows it will need to generate revenues for its owners or sponsors in order to sustain its growth. There are basically three sources of revenue available: member fees, advertising fees, and transaction fees. In the early days of a new electronic community, member fees are to be avoided because they will discourage the accumulation of a critical mass of end users. Advertising fees and transaction fees are sometimes less objectionable to new members of an electronic community.

In fact, a good deal of content for a new electronic community can be generated free of charge by offering to act as an agent for content providers by making their content more widely available over the network. Content providers can also be rewarded by offering them end user profiles and information on exactly who is consuming their content. Partnering with and leveraging the work of content providers is a key to the successful creation of any electronic community including an extranet.

Extranets can grow faster if the sponsoring organization supports this growth with the right set of roles and responsibilities. The right set of roles and responsibilities includes all of the categories shown in Note 10.6. Some of the specific roles needed are that of an executive moderator, community editor, manager of community development, community marketing manager, and a customer services manager.

NOTE 10.6 ————————▶

Extranet Community Roles

✓ Technical

✓ Creative

✓ Editorial

✓ Advertisement

✓ Customer Service

✓ Administration

These roles are somewhat self-explanatory:

► The executive moderator functions much like a moderator at a town meeting to manage an electronic discussion.

► The community editor edits the information made available over an extranet to give it a common look and feel.

► The manager of community development manages development of the technology infrastructure that supports the on-line community.

► The community marketing manager markets the community to both existing and new members of the community.

► The customer service manager ensures that members are happy with their experiences on an extranet.

As you can see from this list, technology-related roles are only a part of the roles that are needed to make an extranet successful. Roles involving editing, publishing, and customer service as well as marketing are also important. In addition, the set of administrative roles namely human resources, finance, legal, etc., common to most organizations are needed.

This is because in a world of electronic communities, loyalty is a two-way street. The existence of the Internet and of multiple extranets means that it will be easy for consumers to shop for the best price or for the product with the product description that best suits their needs. Manufacturers and producers of services can no longer safely assume that their customers do not know market prices or benefits of competing products. Thus, customer loyalty will have to be earned every day on an extranet via the best pricing, quality, or delivery or some combination of these things. Customer loyalty will no longer spring from the superior knowledge of producers as opposed to consumers.

It's important to understand that an on-line community of extranet end users is not exactly like an Internet community of end users. Extranets are unique electronic or virtual communities. Extranets are usually created by commercial organizations interested in pursuing business goals. This means that extranet owners, sponsors, end users, and partners are often much more concerned with issues of profitability, security, privacy, and ownership of intellectual property rights than are Internet end users in general.

This creates some interesting legal and cultural issues for members of an extranet virtual community. For example, most extranets require the use of some sort of encryption technology to ensure privacy and security. However, the United States government places export restrictions on encryption technologies. This means that a United States-based organization that creates an extranet to connect offices in different countries must satisfy the requirements of U.S. export laws in order to legally ship encryption devices overseas. Of course, one way around this might be to simply purchase encryption equipment overseas from suppliers not bound by U.S. laws.

However, this does not solve all of the legal problems confronting designers and implementers of extranets because some countries make the transmission of encrypted data across their boarders illegal. Other countries make the encryption and decryption of any data within their boarders by non-governmental agencies illegal. In many countries the science of cryptology is still regarded as best restricted to use by those government agencies responsible for national defense and security. These issues are explored in greater detail in the chapter on security.

Even if an extranet community consults the right lawyers and implements the right procedures so as to avoid entanglement with the legal issues surrounding security, that community can run afoul of laws requiring it to use local post, telephone, and telegraph organizations to transmit data. Thus, dial back schemes by which one dials to a telephone number inside the United States from a foreign country in order to generate a call back to the foreign country may be a violation of local telecommunications laws. This is because the call coming back from the United States may bypass the local telephone company causing it to lose revenues. Thus, such schemes are violations of criminal and civil laws in some countries. Often these laws are only enforced against companies or organizations that have annoyed the foreign government in some way.

Cultural issues may also create problems for members of a global extranet community. Thus, the heads of on-line services have been prosecuted for transmitting pornography in some countries even though the on-line service was operated as a common carrier and did little or no editing of any on-line materials.

The best way around these legal and cultural issues is to either use one of the larger global Internet Service Providers to worry about these things for you or to hire knowledgeable lawyers and consultants before designing and implementing a global extranet. The unique concerns of extranet communities for security and privacy make the use of such experts mandatory for the avoidance of legal violations.

Unfortunately, most of the people designing and implementing extranets have technical not legal backgrounds and thus are unaware of the legal requirements and cultural complexities surrounding the use of security technologies and dial back or call back technologies.

Potential Conflicts Between Owners or Sponsors of Extranets and End Users

One of the biggest potential conflicts between owners and sponsors of extranets and end users springs from the laissez faire tradition of the Internet and many on-line communities. In fact, many electronic communities started as a rebellion against the straight or traditional culture. Thus, there are bulletin boards and other places in the on-line world where end users believe that all of the products and services offered via an electronic network should be available completely free of charge.

Another reason for potential conflicts between end users and owners or sponsors of extranets is the fact that many on-line communities consist of individuals with a great deal of expertise in and passion for their particular field of interest and thus react with a great deal of hostile expertise to inaccurate or misleading advertising statements. This means that vendors need to be careful in what they say and present over an extranet or risk receiving a flurry of e-mail correcting their claims and that are copied to many customers and business partners. It is the extreme passion and expertise that distinguishes electronic or virtual communities from regular or ordinary communities.

This passion and expertise is a great advantage when it works in favor of the owners of sponsors of extranets but can be extremely painful and damaging to owners and sponsors when it works against them.

This means that owners and sponsors must look to partner with their on-line customers in a much closer sense than they partnered with their real or nonvirtual customers. For example, owners and sponsors of extranets need to listen to the comments and requests of members of the extranet community and answer queries forthrightly, or not at all. The worst thing that owners and sponsors of extranets can do is to promise end users open and honest debate and then not deliver it or worse yet offer spam or unwanted advertising instead!

According to Angela Gunn writing in "Asking for It: What Have You Done to Deserve Spam" (Nov. 1997), positing publicly is an invitation to be harassed with multilevel marketing messages.

Getting to the right level of engagement with end users and members of an extranet community will not be an easy task for extranet owners and sponsors. This is where the owner or sponsor can really benefit from having employees who are "net savvy" and who know how to engage and disengage over an electronic network. Electronic rules of etiquette as described in many books on e-mail and electronic communications can help owners and sponsors reach the right level of engagement with other members of an extranet community.

Things You Can Do Now to Prepare for the Future

Here are some things that organizations and individuals can do now to prepare for the explosive growth of extranets:

▶ Become net savvy or net aware. Reading this book and other books on extranets will help.

▶ Attend industry conferences and listen to people who have designed and implemented extranets. Listen to people who have "been there, done that."

▶ Guard your electronic privacy and security at least as energetically as you do the rest of your rights in a democracy.

▶ Develop a sense of net etiquette or what is good and bad behavior when using an extranet or any other type of electronic network. This will help you get the maximum benefits from any new networking technology.

▶ Don't be afraid to play with new technologies. Play is one of the best ways of learning a new subject.

▶ Develop an awareness of the economic impact of extranets because there is a good chance that this technology will impact your working career.

Chapter Summary

This chapter has discussed:

▶ How corporate, government, and academic research and development are likely to influence extranets.

▶ Technology drivers of extranet growth, i.e., infrastructure and enabling technologies.

▶ Economic drivers of extranet growth.

▶ What creates and makes a community of extranet users grow.

▶ The stages of growth of a community of extranet users.

▶ What extranet owners and sponsors can do to help create and grow a community of extranet users.

▶ Potential conflicts between extranet owners or sponsors and extranet users.

▶ Things that you can do now to prepare for the future.

It is an exciting time to be exploring and using the Internet, intranets, and extranets because these technologies are impacting our careers, our play, and the world around us.

In the next chapter, you will find a decision matrix to help you decide whether an extranet is reliable enough, robust enough, powerful enough, and secure enough to help you meet your business and enterprise wide needs. You may want to modify the matrix to fit your own unique circumstances, but the matrix will get you started on a rational process for designing and implementing as well as deciding whether or not you even want an extranet.

11

Deciding Whether or Not to Implement an Extranet

Chapter Objectives

The two primary objectives of this chapter are to summarize the material previously discussed in this book and to provide you with a matrix which can help you decide whether or not to implement an extranet. The decision matrix in this chapter is not exhaustive so you need to expand it and tailor it to meet your own needs and unique circumstances. However, it does highlight the challenges and solutions that you should consider in your decision making.

The decision matrix and this chapter cover:

- ▶ Why people are excited about extranets
- ▶ Return on Investment Analysis
- ▶ Extranet access
- ▶ Extranet availability and reliability
- ▶ Extranet scalability
- ▶ Extranet security
- ▶ Extranet performance
- ▶ Ease of management
- ▶ Ease of administration
- ▶ Maintainability
- ▶ Future extranet challenges
- ▶ An example of a large successful extranet operation
- ▶ A description of what makes extranets successful

This chapter ends with some brief lists and outlines for those readers who have decided to develop and implement an extranet. Thus, there is a list of extranet design principles, an extranet implementation plan outline, and an extranet support plan outline.

I hope that this information, as well as information from other sources in addition to this book, helps you make wise decisions about developing and implementing extranets.

Here is a decision matrix to get you started in thinking about an extranet project.

The Extranet Decision Matrix

Table 11.1 *Decision Matrix*

	Pros	*Cons*
1. Why the Excitement?	A Chance to Build a Community of Shared Interest and Relationships, to Transact, and Share Dreams and Visions	The Vision has Gotten Ahead of Some of the Reality
2. ROI Analysis	Access to New Markets, Lower Communication and Transaction Costs, Better Relationships with Customers and Business Partners, Greater Geographic and Temporal Reach	Ongoing and One-Time Costs, i.e., Content, Development, Consulting, Software, Training, Hardware, Management, Administrative, Learning Curve, Project Management, Beware of Cost Shifting Instead of Cost Reduction, Other
3. Access	24 × 7 Access to Data and Applications Now Possible from Almost Anywhere; Remote Dial Up and Access from the Small Office Home, Home Office Getting Better	To What Applications and Data at What Price by Whom? Synchronization and Maintenance of User Lists
4. Availability and Reliability	Highly Available and Reliable 24 × 7 Access to Data and Applications Now Possible from Almost Anywhere; Fault Tolerant, and Disaster Recovery Solutions Getting Better	Cost and Effort Required to Design, Implement, Manage, and Administer Distributed Multiserver Systems with Load Balancing and Fail over Capabilities, Cost of Level of Service Agreements, The Cost of Choosing and Implementing Standards

Table 11.1 *Decision Matrix (Continued)*

	Pros	Cons
5. Scalability	Standards Based More Scalable Solutions Increasingly Available	High Cost of Traditional Solutions, i.e., Add More Boxes and Staff, Faster Firewalls, and Networks Needed
6. Security	Now Possible To Protect Data During Transmission and Storage; Real Security Can Now be Better Than Perceived Security	Cost and Effort Required to Design, Implement, Manage, and Administer Firewall, Logging, Usage Tracking Systems
7. Performance	High Performance Solutions Increasingly Available; Expectations Can Be Set Via Careful Benchmark Studies; Colocation Solutions Now Available; Annotation and Editing Tools are Being Optimized for High Performance; Cookies Provide Better Usage Statistics	Large Audio and Video Files Remain a Challenge
8. Ease of Management	Remote Management of Machines Increasingly Available; the Ability to Manage One Thing Instead of Many Things Increasingly Available	Cost and Complexity of Extranet Management Tools; Staffing Ratios Required; Cost of the Inventory Database Required
9. Ease of Administration	Better Tools Available for Administration of End User Accounts, Passwords, and Directories	Cost and Complexity of Extranet Administration Tools; Staffing Ratios Required; Cost of Inventory Database Required
10. Maintainability	Standards and a Good Help Desk Support Operation Help; Good Domain Design Helps; Remote System Upgrade Tools Getting Better	Little Reusability of Code, Low Programmer Productivity
11. Future Challenges	Better Tools, Infrastructure, and Enabling Technologies Increasingly Available; Internet Research and Development Now Focused on Faster Network Backbones, Internet Technologies, Traffic Management and Monitoring; Tools to Enable Internet Commerce, and Implement Better Security	Less and Less Basic R & D is Being Done Because of Budget Constraints. It is Unclear What Technologies Will be Merging When or if Consumers Will Pay for Merging of Television and Merged Technologies. Lack of Basic Educational Skills May Constrain the Use of Extranets

Why the Excitement About Extranets?

If you have read this far you should have a good sense of the answer to this question by now. However, it is worth remembering that even though technology visions sometimes do in fact get out in front of reality, an extranet really is a powerful way for its users to explore common interests, share dreams and visions, build relationships, and transact business. An extranet is a powerful tool for building trust and community. This was mentioned in earlier chapters and more will be said about this later in this chapter.

One of the many reasons why some organizations are excited about extranets is probably wrong or at least likely to get them in trouble as an extranet grows. Extranets are based upon the Internet and Internet technologies, and as lots of people know there's lots of free software available over the Internet that is easy to download, install, and use. Certainly the fact that so much is available for free over the Internet and the fact that it is often easy to install and use is a plus for individual Internet users.

However, this is much less of a plus for organizations. In reality, there is no free lunch on the Internet or anywhere else. Although several e-mail clients are available over the Internet for free (the November 1997 issue of *Internet Computing* reviewed several of these offerings), the providers of these e-mail clients and of free software in general want something in return for their software.

The something that they want is usually user profile information like name, address, telephone number, household income, educational history, and information on household purchasing patterns. They want this information so that they can recruit advertisers who will pay them to e-mail ads to the e-mail accounts of people who receive their free software.

In general, there are two types of advertising for the free software available over the Internet. There are advertising agencies that charge some company a fee to put their ads on a web server with excess capacity. The agency pays a fee to the owner of the web server and lives on the difference between what they charge advertisers to post information to the web server for them and what they pay the owner of the web server to use the server's excess capacity. Everyone who visits the web site gets to see the ads.

In the second type of advertising, an agency collects user profiles and statistics as users visit a web site and sells the information to advertisers so that the advertisers can better focus and target their electronic and traditional ad and marketing campaigns. Many of the firms in web-related business provide one or the other or both types of advertising as well as creative themes, art work and illustration, HTML markup, and media buying as well as hosting.

Life can be difficult for end users who don't want to receive Internet-based advertising.

In the case of e-mail ads directed to end user e-mail accounts, filtering will not prevent unwanted e-mail if the sender uses different accounts each time it sends its e-mail ads. End user e-mail addresses can be recorded by robots that scan e-mail headers, thus making it difficult for an end user to maintain an electronic "unlisted e-mail address." E-mail address skimming software is improving rapidly and making it easier than ever for electronic advertisers to pull addresses from end user e-mails for use in bulk e-mail ad campaigns.

Some people are willing to exchange information for free software and use free e-mail clients to set up e-mail accounts for personal communications. The free e-mail accounts complement their e-mail accounts at work that are used for business communications. These individuals don't mind receiving unsolicited ads e-mailed to their personal e-mail accounts. Often, these e-mail clients are browser based so that they run on multiple platforms.

Some providers of "free e-mail clients" via the Internet also promise unlimited lifetime storage for old e-mail and attachments. Usually, this offer disappears as the provider grows and has to provide ever-larger volumes of storage for e-mail and attachments.

Enterprises and organizations are less likely to benefit from the software available for free over the Internet than are individual users. This is because free software does not usually scale up well as the volume of transactions and number of users increases, often comes without maintenance and upgrade guarantees or commitments, and does not have all of the security features and functionality of enterprise class solutions. Of course, there are exceptions to this statement, but in general much of the software available for free over the Internet was never intended to run mission-critical applications like payroll, order management, billing, and customer service especially for large enterprises.

There are plenty of good reasons to get excited about extranets without getting carried away by the "free software and things" available over the Internet. Most extranets are implemented by organizations that need to consider the scalability, maintainability, upgradability, manageability, and security characteristics of their networks.

A Return on Investment Analysis for Extranets

A great deal can be said on this topic. However, the most important thing to remember is that for many end users an extranet represents a totally new experience. This means that their requirements for an effective extranet need to be constructed rather than discovered.

This lack of extranet experience on the part of new extranet end users means that extranet developers and implementers cannot validate extranet requirements by simply asking potential extranet end users what they want because end users who have never experienced an extranet or something like it before cannot know what they want in an extranet. Instead, effective validation of extranet requirements is likely to proceed along the lines of first identifying a problem that end users care about and that an extranet might solve, the objectives of the proposed solution, and how an extranet might be used to meet these objectives.

Demonstrations to end users of quickly and easily developed prototype systems is a good way to validate extranet requirements because this provides developers and implementers with immediate feedback based on end users interaction and experiences with at least a minimal extranet system. In this scenario, end users don't have to guess what an extranet might be like and might do for them instead they get to actually experience at least a minimal extranet system. Thus, the most effective extranet return on investment analyses usually involve the building of prototypes and demo systems, the showing of prototypes and demo systems, and the discussions that follow along from showing prototypes and demo systems.

Extranet Access

The future of extranet access like the future of Internet access or the future of intranet access is likely to be one of easy access from anywhere via ubiquitous and easy to use devices that communicate over a very sophisticated network infrastructure with a powerful and complex backend. In other words, extranet access is likely to follow models set by a water system, or telephone system. Access to both of these systems is widely available via easy to use devices that are supported by very strong network infrastructure and by a powerful and complex backend. In fact much application functionality and data is moving from the desktop to web servers, database servers, and other backend or back room machines. Presentation logic and applications like word processing and spreadsheets that are normally used by one user at a time remain on desktop machines.

It is important to remember that effective extranet access is a function of more than just good technology. It also a function of good access policies and procedures as well as of consistency with local laws and culture.

In some cultures extranet owners and sponsors are expected not to share certain kinds of information. Thus, the sharing of a list of bank customers is a highly illegal act in some countries but is a common business and advertising practice in other countries.

In some countries a variety of competing telecommunications vendors exist and in other countries there is a legal requirement to use the government-sponsored and monopolistic telecommunications provider. Thus, effective extranet access like effective extranet security involves a great deal more than the latest technology although it is the technology that makes an extranet possible in the first place.

Availability and Reliability

Great progress has been made in the technology to make extranets highly reliable and available. Thus multiple servers, round robin domain name address resolution, fail over and fail back mechanisms, and partitioning of data types across multiple servers have lead to some highly available and reliable extranets. This chapter includes an example and description of such an extranet operation. See the section below on A Global Extranet Environment.

Scalability

Significant scalability issues remain for extranets and firewalls. Some large extranet operations have attempted to scale up by buying more boxes and staff to run the additional boxes. These operations are now running out of real estate and space in which to put the additional boxes and staff.

In contrast to the traditional approach to attempting to solve the scalability problem by buying more boxes and hiring more staff, some of the newer operating systems provide for consolidation of many servers to fewer servers running the new software with advanced management and administration functionality. This is likely to be the trend in the future as extranet owners and sponsors seek to solve their scalability and growth problems without buying more and more real estate.

Extranet Security

Good extranet security is like effective extranet access because good security depends upon effective policies and procedures and consistency with local laws and culture as much as it depends upon good technology. Moreover, extranet owners and sponsors need to be aware of the laws regulating the import, export, and implementation of cryptosystems.

In addition, perceived security is likely to be as important as real security to extranet owners and sponsors. After all, end users are not likely to trust an extranet with personal and financial information unless they perceive it to be secure. Thus, a successful extranet is in fact and in perception secure.

Performance

Extranet performance is improving and is likely to improve even more in the future with the emergence of faster network backbone and traffic control technologies. Although sending large audio and video files across an extranet today is difficult, better software tools, standards, and faster hardware is leading to impressive performance improvements.

Many of today's performance challenges are due to network bandwidth constraints, long execution times in multilevel interpretive environments, varying or nonexistent standards, and incompatible plug-ins. The network bandwidth constraints limit the sending and receiving of large multimedia files. Long execution times often apply to multilevel interpretive JAVA environments. Lack of standards drive up the cost of technology and limit its usefulness in a business environment.

Although performance limitations are most visible when dealing with large multimedia tools and files, it's not really performance that keeps multimedia technology from being deployed in businesses today. Instead, it's the fact that multimedia technology has not yet been combined with business-oriented logic to generate business applications that add to the bottom line. High-performance multimedia technology will be taken far more seriously and be much more widely adopted when it has validated itself in important business applications. Better performance is coming, and multimedia business applications need to be developed to make use of the extra performance.

Extranet Management and Administration

Although the tools and technology to do this are getting better, it is still a very significant challenge for a large extranet operation. This is especially the case if different hardware and operating systems are involved and tools are not integrated. Thus, cross platform and integrated tools are needed here.

Maintainability

Maintainability like management and administration can be hard for owners and sponsors of extranets because of the multivendor and extremely heterogeneous environments of many extranets. Browsers and JAVA code can be extremely useful to designers and implementers of extranets because these two technologies are platform independent.

You can think of a browser as a platform independent client and of JAVA code as platform independent application code sent from a server to a desktop device for execution. Thus, a browser will run on any desktop machine and applications written in JAVA code will execute on any desktop machine. This means that designers and implementers of extranets can avoid a wide range of compatibility and interoperability problems by choosing to use browsers and JAVA code in their extranet designs and implementations.

By using the Distributed Component Object Method from Microsoft or the Common Object Request Broker Architecture from the Open Management Group extranet designers and implementers can develop language independent objects or libraries of software that can be reused many times by many different programmers. This should improve programmer productivity and thereby lower software maintenance and enhancement costs for owners and sponsors of extranets.

Future Challenges for Extranets

Although a great deal of applied research and development is being done on everything from faster Internet backbones to better Internet traffic control tools to the merger of Internet and television technology, basic research is being decreased because of governmental and industrial budget cuts. In addition, it appears that many workers are graduating from schools without even basic reading, writing, and mathematical skills. Whether these constraints will hurt extranet implementations and deployments in the future is an unanswered question at the present time.

However, because of the large amount of applied extranet research being done at this time, it looks as though extranets and the Internet will continue to grow for some time to come. To help you better understand the issues and solutions listed in the extranet decision matrix, we'll discuss an example of a very large and successful extranet implementation next.

A Global Extranet Environment

One of the best ways to understand and evaluate what is involved in designing and implementing an extranet is to look at what some of the largest extranet designers and implementers have done and to understand their environments. The providers of global and remote network and system management services are a good model to look at because these companies in effect have been operating extranets or extranet like networks for many years.

The first thing one notices in looking at these operations is that they are selectively open or porous. Their firewalls and security systems cannot do general blocking. Instead, they must allow their customers who run many different types of protocols and systems 24 hours a day and 7 days a week access. In addition, these operations make use of high-speed extranets and of 45 megabit and even of 100 megabit backbone connections which often push firewall and server load balancing technologies to their limits.

Availability like access and performance is a major issue for these large operators of extranets. Load balancing and separation of content across multiple servers via round robin domain name server address resolution and other procedures is a key need of these firms.

In addition, these operations face ongoing scalability issues. The traditional solution to problems of scalability and growth has been to add an additional box along with an additional system administrator and manager to manage the box. This traditional solution rapidly encounters limits as extranet owners and sponsors run out of floor space and real estate to hold all of the additional boxes and staff. Newer solutions to the scalability problem incorporate modularization and componentization in order to overcome limits of so many connections per box.

For legal, business, and security reasons, providers of remote network and system management services maintain huge audit logs that sometimes consume gigabytes of computer memory. This fact creates an enormous need for tools to scan the audit logs in real time and to generate alarms when network or system intruders are encountered. So far, there are relatively few of these tools on the market. Thus, audit logs need to be visually scanned by human beings if the audit logs are to be used at all.

In addition, the whole area of remote system and network management through tunnels is undergoing rapid evolution. Therefore, companies attempting to do system and network management from a headquarters office to a remote branch office can attempt to do so via a secure encrypted tunnel that passes through the firewalls at both offices and that connects a network. These companies also need a system manager at the headquarters office to manage the machines and systems in the remote office.

Although the tunnel penetrates both the firewalls of the remote branch office and of the headquarters office, the tunnel is only available to the addresses specified for each end of the tunnel. Unfortunately this solution is not quite as good as it sounds because addresses can be spoofed or impersonated; thus giving an intruder access to the tunnel.

Firewall vendors and others continue to do a large amount of research and development to address this and other security issues like authentication and nonrepudiation as well. However, security remains a rapidly evolving area for owners or sponsors of extranets.

Most computer security experts say that 80% of computer and network security problems originate inside and not outside an organization. Thus, contrary to popular belief, most computer and network security problems within organizations do not originate from the Internet after all. Instead, they come from different groups and individuals within the organization itself.

Sometimes the problem is that one division or group of an organization is seeing things that another division or group does not want them to see. To solve this and other security problems, firewall vendors are talking about placing a firewall on every single computer both to limit where information can be sent to from that platform and to protect the operating system, applications, and data on that platform from intrusion. In fact, a few firewall vendors are even talking about placing a firewall in every application.

The major challenge to overcome in implementing this type of desktop firewall functionality is management and administration of potentially thousands of standalone firewalls. Although a solution to this challenge is not yet in sight, this is clearly where firewall technology is headed. The evolution and emergence of desktop firewalls, and of the firewall on every computer or in every application, is likely to increase the pressure and need for well thought out and articulated information security policies and procedures.

The movement of firewalls to every desktop reflects the ongoing pendulum swing between centralized and distributed models of computing that periodically sweeps through the computing industry. Some commentators have even described the World Wide Web as nothing more than a return of applications and data to the mainframe or at least to a server.

From the standpoint of security alone, highly centralized applications and data are easier to secure than are widely distributed data.

Indeed, banks have opted to store cash in a highly secure centralized location known as a "vault or safe" while making cash widely accessible from automated teller machines. The mainframe dumb terminal model or single tier client server model was very effective in terms of security, availability, management, and administration.

What drove people toward distributed models of computing or multi-tier client server models was a need for modularization; componentization; separation of data, programs, and presentation; and for adaptable systems. Large extranet deployments often centralize mission-critical data and applications for purposes of security while separating different data types across multiple servers to increase reliability and availability. Thus, large extranet deployments are often combinations of centralized and distributed systems and architectures! Access from easy to use and ubiquitous devices from all over the world is also usually part of a large extranet deployment.

Branding is a big part of perceived rather than actual security on an extranet. Thus, extranets with names associated with large, stable, and trusted organizations will often be perceived by end users as being more secure than extranets associated with start up or brand new and untrusted organizations. Therefore, some extranets have dramatically increased usage statistics by choosing a new name that people associate with secure and trusted organizations.

Actually, not everyone needs the high levels of security sought by very large corporate providers of extranets. Indeed, some extranet owners or sponsors are content to simply restrict their extranet traffic to the network of a particular Internet Service Provider and to rely upon that Internet Service Provider to provide at least minimal security. Others are content to have their secure tunnels start and stop at firewalls and network access servers and to rely upon the security provided by their internal networks once data reaches a firewall or network access server. In fact, a security threat analysis should be done to determine what information needs protection and how this can best be done.

Although everyone does not need an identical level of security, many extranet end users desire a single point of log on, authentication, and entitlement. Many end users balk at being asked to remember different desktop, network, and server passwords. They often attempt to get around this security requirement by choosing identical passwords for their desktop, network, and servers. A single point of log on, authentication, and entitlement is a firm requirement for global extranets that deal with roaming or traveling end users.

In addition to the security challenges of owning or sponsoring extranets, there are standards issues as well. As described in an earlier chapter on security, nonproprietary tunneling protocols are emerging. However, at the present time almost all tunneling implementations are actually based on proprietary rather than nonproprietary standards.

Ease of deployment, maintainability, upgradability, and platform independence are additional goals and characteristics of large extranet deployments and operations.

The possibility of sending Windows upgrades down the wire just like JAVA code applications can be sent down the wire is likely to be a boon to such extranet deployments and operations.

In spite of these issues and concerns, it is important to note that large providers of remote system and network management services over extranets are, in fact, successful companies who derive much of their revenue by successfully using extranet technology to reach and service their customers. Without the global reach provided by extranets, these companies would serve far smaller markets, have less revenue, and have higher cost structures. Extranets are not just competitive advantage for these large services companies they are a necessity.

What Makes an Extranet Successful?

Besides good technology, great content, and good project management, adding a human touch to what has traditionally been a very high tech environment often makes the difference between success and failure for an extranet. When visitors become fully engaged participants contributing their content and work product while telling their friends and colleagues about the many advantages of an extranet, an extranet is well on the path to success. This is because a self feeding and closed loop of success has been created in which better content generates still more and better content and more end users generate still more end users who contribute more and better content of their own to an extranet.

When properly managed and nurtured, such an extranet virtual community generates lower costs and growing revenues for its owners and sponsors. This is because fully engaged end users are far more likely than surfers or casual visitors to become consumers of services and products as well as content generators. It is not unusual for successful communities to be growing by as many as 2,000 new users per day. Moreover, these new users often return to visit the on-line community as many as three times per week.

These on-line communities have not only mastered the art of attracting and engaging new members, they are often viewed by their members as a "social happening" or "in thing."

In some ways, it easier for a commercial extranet owner or sponsor to build an on-line community than it is for a less commercial owner or sponsor. This is because commercial owners and sponsors by their very nature are usually focused on specific markets and interests, and focus on a specific interest is the fundamental reason why virtual communities form in the first place. Without a specific focus, there is little or no chance of creating and growing an on-line community.

Thus, the most important thing that an extranet owner or sponsor can do is to allow participants and administrators to interact easily, conveniently, and frequently. In other words, a well-designed and implemented e-mail system is a critical success factor for an extranet. Thus, customers, sales representatives, customer service representatives, and technical support representatives should all be linked by an effective and efficient e-mail system.

However, e-mail tends to be private communication between limited numbers of people. Thus, successful extranet communities also require technology for collaboration between many people as well as open forums and bulletin boards or chat sessions. Public message conferences can be open and shared but may well require a moderator to keep the discussion focused on the goals of an extranet community. The goal should be a positive and informative discussion rather than a negative or insulting discussion.

Public message conferences enable extranet members to work together to build solutions and content on-line and lower the cost of communicating new content to remote end users. There is no hardcopy or CD-ROMs to develop and mail out. Most importantly of all, public conferences on an extranet give new members a reason to connect an extranet and remain connected for some time. This can be crucial to creating a sense of community in new on-line members.

Chat rooms or user to user communication through computers are a great way to build a sense of community and identity because if managed well they can build a sense of common interest and trust between members of an extranet community. Chat rooms and chat room discussions can also help an extranet community refine its focus and its content; thereby making it more and more attractive to both new and old members.

Often a new extranet will need to be seeded with content. Getting extranet members to attractive and interesting content quickly is what an extranet is all about. Thus, seeding a new extranet with effective content is a mandatory requirement for the owners and sponsors of a new extranet. The best way to do this is to talk with people who share the same interests and needs as the target audience for an extranet and ensure that from the moment it opens for business an extranet can meet at least some of these interests and needs.

Often a hint or touch of controversy can stimulate a new discussion group and encourage new end users to jump in and join the discussion. This has to be managed, but can be an effective way to engage new members and to start the content generation process from new members of an extranet community. The presence of experts and celebrities on-line is another tool that can be used to engage new members to kick start a new extranet community.

However, successful extranets do more than seed content, they also feed or nurture a new extranet community by encouraging ongoing participation. Thus, they find some way to reduce the usual 10 or 100 to 1 standard ratio of casual visitors to web sites to participants in web sites. As an extranet community grows it develops a set of regular participants who become the backbone of the extranet community. Often these regulars are a good source of moderators and discussion leaders who can complement the work of and off-load work from regular staff.

In addition, successful extranet web sites are often perceived by end users to be attractive in appearance, highly graphical and colorful, easy to navigate, full of exciting content, well managed, and high performance. All of these perceptions help attract new visitors to the web site and retain visitors once they arrive. See Figure 11.1 for a summary of the properties of successful extranets.

The most successful extranets out there are thriving on-line communities attracting and engaging new members and old members constantly.

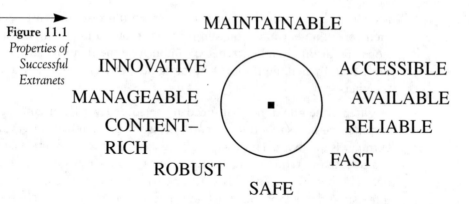

Figure 11.1
Properties of Successful Extranets

MAINTAINABLE

INNOVATIVE   ACCESSIBLE

MANAGEABLE   AVAILABLE

CONTENT–   RELIABLE
RICH

ROBUST   FAST

SAFE

Some Useful Lists, Tables, and Outlines

The following lists and outlines are brief summaries of issues and solutions discussed in much greater detail in earlier chapters of this book. You can use them to refresh your memory of what you have read and as raw material for developing your own more detailed extranet designs and plans. Check the index if you want more detailed information on anything listed.

Table 11.2 *A List of Extranet Architecture and Design Principles*

1. No Single Point of Failure
2. Multiple Servers Used
3. Different Data Types Spread Across Multiple Servers
4. Subnet, Network Access Server to Network Access Server, or Desktop to Desktop Tunnels
5. Some Variant of Round Robin Domain Name Server Address Resolution and Intelligent Querying of Servers Used to Enhance Availability, Reliability, and Performance
6. Performance Enhanced Via Fast Network Backbones and Enabling Technologies
7. Strong Crypto Systems Used to Protect Data During Storage and Transmission
8. Strong Authentication Systems Used to Validate End Users, Clients, and Servers
9. Strong Passwords Chosen, Managed, and Often Changed
10. Firewalls and Virus Scanners Used to Separate Trusted and Untrusted Networks
11. Extensive Logging of Usage and Performance Statistics as Well as of End User Profiles
12. Periodic and Detailed Review of Logs By Security and Network Managers

Table 11.2 *A List of Extranet Architecture and Design Principles*

13. Full Compliance with National and Local Laws and Customs
14. Periodic Upgrades to Infrastructure and Enabling Technologies Planned For
15. End Users and Others Trained in Extranet or Network Etiquette
16. Threat Analysis, Security, and Information Policies and Procedures in Place

Table 11.3 *An Extranet Implementation Plan Outline*

1. Pilot and Early Prototype Plan in Place
2. A Description of the Membership of an Extranet Community
3. Training Available for Extranet End Users, Help Desk Support Personnel, Roaming Users, Extranet Managers and Administrators
4. Project Management in Place with Milestones and Growth Plans
5. Content Developers and Editors in Place
6. Third Party Vendor Support in Place
7. Extranet Feedback Mechanisms and Customer Service Representatives in Place
8. A Management Reporting or Accountability Plan in Place
9. A Risk Management Plan in Place

Table 11.4 *An Extranet Support Plan Outline*

This is really a detailed Help Desk Support Plan that covers:
1. Hours of Coverage
2. Numbers and Types of Help Desk Support Specialists Available
3. Help Desk Support Tools Available
4. Problem Escalation Process
5. Problem Triage Process
6. Level of Service Agreements and Guarantees
7. Support Plans for Mobile and Roaming End Users

Chapter Summary

By now, I hope that I have convinced you that extranets if well designed, implemented, maintained, and understood, are ready for prime time deployment. They are likely to be crucial to business success in the future. I also hope that I have convinced you that extranets are not "just information systems" or "technology" opportunities and challenges.

Much of the road to success is social, legal, and cultural; and therefore, requires heavy participation and support by stakeholders and business partners. Extranets are far more than the sum of the technologies that make them up. Successful extranets are thriving on-line or virtual communities of stakeholders and business partners. They are collections of people bound together by common interests, relationships, shared visions, and shared transactions. I wish you success in your journey along the path to developing and nourishing your on-line community or extranet!

This chapter has covered:

▶ Why people are excited about extranets

▶ Return on Investment Analysis

▶ Extranet access

▶ Extranet availability and reliability

▶ Extranet scalability

▶ Extranet security

▶ Extranet performance

▶ Ease of management

▶ Ease of administration

▶ Maintainability

▶ Future extranet challenges

▶ An example of a large successful extranet operation

▶ A description of what makes extranets successful

You can expand upon the lists, outlines, tables, and discussion here to develop and decide upon your own extranet designs and implementations. For further information look at the Bibliography.

Good luck with your own extranet related efforts in the future!

Bibliography

Books

Baker, Richard H. *Extranets: The Complete Sourcebook.* New York: McGraw-Hill, 1997.

Boar, Bernard, H. *The Art of Strategic Planning for Information Technology Crafting Strategy for the 90s.* New York: John Wiley and Sons, 1993.

Cambell-Kelly, Martin, and Aspray, William. *Computer: A History of the Information Machine.* New York: Basic Books, 1996.

Covill, Randall J. *Migrating to the Intranet and Microsoft Exchange.* Boston: Digital Press, 1997.

Denning, Peter J., and Metcalfe, Robert M. *Beyond Calculation: The Next Fifty Years of Computing.* New York: Copernicus, Springer-Verlag, 1997.

Dertouzos, Michael. *What Will Be: How the World of Information Will Change Our Lives.* New York: HarperEdge, HarperCollins Pub., 1997.

Dixit, Avinash K., and Nalebuff, Barry J. *Thinking Strategically: The Competitive Edge in Business, Politics, and Everyday Life.* New York: W. W. Norton and Company, 1991.

Farley, Marc, Stearns, Tom, and Hsu, Jeffry. *LAN Times Guide to Security and Data Integrity.* Berkeley, CA: McGraw-Hill, 1996.

Freedman, David H., and Mann, Charles C. *@Large: The Strange Case of the World's Biggest Internet Invasion.* New York: Simon and Schuster, 1997.

Hafner, Katie, and Lyon, Matthew. *Where Wizards Stay Up Late: The Origins of the Internet.* New York: Simon and Schuster, 1996.

Hagel III, John, and Armstrong, Arthur G. *Net Gain: Expanding Markets Through Virtual Communities.* Boston: Harvard Business School Press, 1997.

Hughes Jr., Larry J. *Actually Useful Internet Security Techniques.* Indianapolis, IN: New Riders Publishing, 1995.

Kalakota, Ravi, and Whinston, Andrew B. *Frontiers of Electronic Commerce.* New York: Addison-Wesley, 1996.

Kimmons, Robert L. *Project Management Basics: A Step By Step Approach.* New York: Marcel Dekker Inc., 1990.

Martin, James. Cybercorp: *The New Business Revolution.* New York: The American Management Association, 1996.

Martin, James, and Leben, Joe. *Strategic Information Planning Methodologies,* 2nd Ed. Englewood Cliffs, NJ: Prentice-Hall, 1989.

Quinn, Robert E. *Deep Change: Discovering the Leader Within.* San Francisco, CA: Jossey-Bass, Inc., 1996.

Shenk, David. *Data Smog: Surviving the Information Glut.* New York: HarperEdge, HarperCollins Pub., 1997.

Sun-Tzu. *The Art of Warfare: Translated with an Introduction and Commentary by Roger Ames.* New York: Ballantine Books, 1993.

Tapscott, Don. *The Digital Economy: Promise and Peril in the Age of Networked Intelligence.* New York: McGraw-Hill, 1996.

Watterson, Karen. *Client/Server Technology for Managers.* New York: Addison-Wesley, 1995.

Wolman, W. and Colamosca. *The Judas Economy: The Triumph of Capital and the Betrayal of Work.* New York: Addison-Wesley, 1997.

Yourdon, Edward. *Death March: The Complete Software Developer's Guide to Surviving "Mission Impossible" Projects.* Upper Saddle River, NJ: Prentice-Hall Inc., 1997.

Yourdon, Edward. *Object-Oriented Systems Design: An Integrated Approach.* Upper Saddle River, NJ: Prentice-Hall Inc., 1994.

Journals

Dern, Daniel P. "Protect or Serve," *WebMaster* (Apr. 1997).

Dowd, Ann Reilly. "How to Protect Your Privacy," *Money Magazine* (Aug. 1997).

Gunn, Angela. "Asking for It: What Have You Done to Deserve Spam," *Internet Computing* (Ziff-Davis Publishers) 2, no. 11 (Nov. 1997): 49.

Pallato, John. "HP Web Tool Monitors Printers," *Internet Computing* (Ziff-Davis Publishers) 2, no. 11 (Nov. 1997): 123.

Pallato, John. "Building the Ties That Bind," *Internet Computing* (Ziff-Davis Publishers) 3, no. 1 (Jan. 1998): 67.

Pang, Albert. "E-Commerce Bonanza: Is It Real or Imagined?" *Internet Computing* (Ziff-Davis Publishers) 3, no. 3 (Mar. 1998): 70.

Shotland, Nicole, and Taschek, James. "Security Crackdown," *Internet Computing* (Ziff-Davis Publishers) 3, no. 3 (Mar. 1998): 31.

Taschek, James. "Taking the Internet Private," *Internet Computing* (Ziff-Davis Publishers) 3, no. 1 (Jan. 1998): 71.

Taschek, James. "A Well-Balanced Web," *Internet Computing* (Ziff-Davis Publishers) 3, no. 3 (Mar. 1998): 85.

Van Name, Mark, and Catchings, Bill. "Your Best Performance Investment," *Internet Computing* (Ziff-Davis Publishers) 3, no. 3 (Mar. 1998): 53.

"Website Makeovers E-commerce: Four to Watch," *Internet Computing* (Ziff-Davis Publishers) 3, no. 3 (Mar. 1998): 76.

Professional Conferences

DCI Client Server World. Boston, MA, 1997.

Networld-Interop. Atlanta, GA, and Las Vegas, NV, Spring and Fall 1997.

NT-Intranet World. San Francisco, CA, 1997.

Index

Page numbers followed by "f" denote figures; "t" denote tables.

A

Access, to extranet and Internet
  case study of, 76–77
  by casual users, 39–40
  companies that provide, 58t
  cost variations, 41
  difficulties associated with, 36–37
  forecasting methods, 59
  future of, 182–183
  growth of, 56t–59t, 56–61
  low speed, 40
  by mobile users, 38
  regional differences, 40–41
  remote
    business policies and procedures
        available via, 66
    business-related need for, 64–66
    cost savings associated with, 62
    dedicated systems, 69–70
    distribution programs for, 62–63
    enterprise class solutions, 69
    global
      description of, 73–76
      difficulties associated with,
          74–75
      solutions for, 76
    help desk support, 68
    hybrid systems, 69–70
    methods of
      dial up, 66–68
      extended local area network,
          68–69
      modem, 67–68
    multiple channels for, 69
    reasons for, 61–62

    stages of, 63–64
    for telecommuters, 61
    summary of, 77–78
    user lists, 72
Advertising, 180–181
America Online, 10, 75
Application gateways, for Internet security,
    21–22
Application programming interfaces, for
        Internet security, 22
Architecture
  adaptive systems, 42
  client server-distributed, 42
  overview of, 192t–193t
  standards, 43–44
  of virtual private network, 41–43
  web-based front end types, 42
Audio/visual files, transfer of
  collaborative computing for, 131–132
  improved methods for, 128–129
  requirements for, 127t
  tools for, 130
Authentication
  description of, 100–101
  host to host, 107
  individual characteristics, 101–102
  password
    challenge response procedures, 105
    description of, 70t, 102–103
    employee education, 103
    end user use, 104
    implementation methods, 104
  possession of object, 101–102
  third party trust model, 106–107
  types of, 101

B

Back-up, 148
Bandwidth allocation control protocol (BACP), 71t
Benchmark testing, of extranets, 85–87
Bulletin boards, 167

C

Casual users, 37
CGI programs. *See* Common gateway interface
          programs
Challenge handshake authentication protocol
          (CHAP), 70t
Chat rooms, 190
Cisco Systems, 76–77
Collapsed backbone, 132
Common gateway interface programs, 23
Common object request broker architecture
    description of, 83
    intelligent querying using, 88
Communication technologies, 3–4, 4t
Computers. *See* Personal computers
Confidentiality, 96
Cryptographic solutions, for extranet security
    description of, 108–109
    encryption, 108–109
    exportation of, 114
    factors that affect strength of, 110
    public key, 109
    secret key, 109

D

Data encryption standard (DES), 111
Demilitarized zones (DMZ), 53
Disaster recovery, 147–149
Distributed component object method
    description of, 83
    intelligent querying using, 88

E

E-mail
    ads, 180–181
    private nature of, 190
    security of, 17
Encryption technology
    definition of, 108–109
    description of, 50
    implementation of, 51
    international differences in legality of, 75

End users
    community roles, 171–172
    conflicts, 174–175
    extranet owner participation in growth of, 170–171
    growth stages, 169–170
    increases in, 166–168
    loyalty, 172
Extranet. *See also* Virtual private network
    academia influences on, 162–163
    access. *See* Access
    administration
        business-driven approach to policies and
            procedures, 155–156
        cost savings of, 151–152
        definition of, 140
        domain designs, 152–153
        future of, 184–185
        help desk support, 156–160
        permissions, 153–154
        sharing of costs, 154–155
        user accounts, 153
    advertising on, 180–181
    architecture. *See* Architecture
    availability and reliability
        benchmark testing, 85–87
        colocation solution for, 88–89
        design of, 84–85
        example of, 91
        expectations for, 85–87
        external hosting solutions, 88–89
        future of, 183
        implementation of, 84–85, 193t
        latency of, 86
        performance goals, 85–87
        product solutions, 92
        recommendations for, 90
        round robin domain name server techniques,
            87–88
        wide area networking peer connections, 89–90
    benefits of, 180–181
    business challenges for, 72–73
    commercial transactions using, 52–53
    corporate influences on, 162–163
    cost savings of, 151–152
    costs of, 30–31
    decision matrix, 178t–179t
    definition of, 2–3
    economic drivers of, 166
    economic impact of, 60t

end users of
  community roles, 171–172
  conflicts, 174–175
  extranet owner participation in growth of,
      170–171
  growth stages, 169–170
  increases in, 166–168
  loyalty, 172
future challenges for, 185–186
global
  access considerations for, 73–76
  environment, description of, 186–189
government influences on, 162–163
growth of, factors that affect, 166–168
infrastructure
  challenges for expanding, 60t
  description of, 164–165
Internet as
  benefits of, 25–26, 31t
  cost drivers
    application gateways, 21–22
    application programming interfaces, 21–22
    client server configurations, 11t, 11–13
    performance, 22–23
    security, 15–22
    tunneling options, 19–21
    web-enabled application development,
        23–25
  lesson learned from using, 5t–6t
management of
  back-up strategies, 144
  database, 142–143
  definition of, 140
  description of, 185
  disaster recovery scenarios, 147–148
  end user involvement, 142
  fault tolerance considerations, 147–148
  firewall use, 142
  future of, 184–185
  inventory, 142–143
  monitoring methods, 147
  name resolution to TCP/IP server addresses,
      145
  remote software upgrades, 143–145
  sizing, 149
  staffing ratios, 140–141
  tools for, 146–147
performance
  audio/visual files

collaborative computing, 131–132
  tools for, 130
  transfer methods, 128–129
  transfer requirements for, 127t
bandwidth and quality control predictability,
    solutions for, 131
considerations for, 45–47
description of, 123–124
file compression techniques, 129–130
future of, 184
gateway solution, 133–135
recommended investment for, 135–136
routing system limitations, 127–128
usage and, relationship between, 124–125
protocols, 70–71
reasons for joining, 168
recommendations for, 175
return on investment analysis, 26t–30t, 182
revenue, 30–31, 171
risks of, 72–73
schematic representation of, 3f
security. See Security
success of, factors that influence,
    189–191
technological drivers of, 163–164

F
Fat clients, vs. thin clients, 41–42, 44
Fat server, vs. thin server, 44–45
File compression, 129–130
Firewalls
  description of, 16–17, 51–52, 114–115
  gateways, 115–117
  in global extranets, 186–187
  host based, 117
  indications for, 20
  packet filter, 115
  performance effects of, 22–23, 46
  security attacks, 16–17, 19t, 51–52
  virus transfer across, 51–52

G
Gateway computers, for enhancing extranet
    performance, 133–135
Global access, to extranet and Internet
  description of, 73–76
  difficulties associated with, 74–75
  solutions for, 76

H

Hash function, 110
Help desk support, 68, 156–160, 193t

I

International data encryption algorithm, 112
Internet
    access. *See* Access
    companies doing business on, 57t
    confidentiality concerns, 96
    creation of, 8
    as extranet. *See also* Extranet
        benefits of, 25–26, 31t
        cost drivers
            application gateways, 21–22
            application programming interfaces, 21–22
            client server configurations, 11t, 11–13
            performance, 22–23
            security, 15–22
            tunneling options, 19–21
            web-enabled application development, 23–25
    growth of, 15, 47–48
    reliability considerations, 47
    return on investment analysis templates, 26t–30t
    scalability of
        description of, 47–49
        future of, 183
    as virtual private network
        cost drivers
            growth and scalability, 15
            Internet access, 9–10
        description of, 2–3
Internet Service Providers
    competition among, 10
    description of, 10, 58t
    services offered by, 10
Internetworking protocol (IPSec), 71t
ISP. *See* Internet Service Providers

J

JPEG files, 129

L

LAN. *See* Local area network
Layer 2 forwarding protocol, 70t
Layer 2 tunneling protocol, 70t
L2FP. *See* Layer 2 forwarding protocol
L2TP. *See* Layer 2 tunneling protocol
Local area network, 68–69

M

Management, of extranet
    back-up strategies, 144
    database, 142–143
    definition of, 140
    disaster recovery scenarios, 147–148
    end user involvement, 142
    fault tolerance considerations, 147–148
    firewall use, 142
    inventory, 142–143
    monitoring methods, 147
    name resolution to TCP/IP server addresses, 145
    remote software upgrades, 143–145
    sizing, 149
    staffing ratios, 140–141
    tools for, 146–147
MLP. *See* Multi-link protocol
MLP+. *See* Multi-link protocol +
Mobile users
    access difficulties for, 38
    description of, 38
Modem, for remote access, 67
MPEG files, 129
Multi-link protocol, 71t
Multi-link protocol +, 71t

N

Network
    host-to-host transfers, 39
    security protection, 39

O

Online service providers. *See* Internet Service Providers
Open systems interconnection, 18t–19t

P

Packet filters, for firewalls, 115
PAP. *See* Password authentication protocol
Password authentication protocol
    challenge response procedures, 105
    description of, 70t, 102–103
    employee education, 103
    end user use, 104
    implementation methods, 104
PCs. *See* Personal computers
Peer to peer protocol, 9
Performance, extranet
    audio/visual files

collaborative computing, 131–132
tools for, 130
transfer methods, 128–129
transfer requirements for, 127t
bandwidth and quality control predictability,
solutions for, 131
considerations for, 45–47
description of, 123–124
file compression techniques, 129–130
future of, 184
gateway solution, 133–135
recommended investment for, 135–136
routing system limitations, 127–128
usage and, relationship between,
124–125
Personal computers
net, 11t, 12
upgrading of, 38
Point of Presence sharing, 10
Point to point tunneling protocol, 70t
POP sharing. See Point of Presence sharing
Power users, 36–37
PPP. See Peer to peer protocol
Programmer productivity, 45
Protocols
Bandwidth allocation control protocol (BACP),
71t
Challenge handshake authentication protocol
(CHAP), 70t
Internetworking protocol (IPSec), 71t
Layer 2 forwarding protocol (L2FP), 70t
Layer 2 tunneling protocol (L2TP), 70t
Multi-link protocol (MLP), 71t
Multi-link protocol + (MLP+), 71t
Password authentication protocol (PAP), 70t
Point to point tunneling protocol (PPTP), 70t
Proxy gateways, 115–117
PPTP. See Point to point tunneling protocol

R
Random arrays of inexpensive disks, 148
Relay gateways, 115–117
Reliability, of Internet, 47
Remote access, to extranet and Internet
business policies and procedures available via, 66
business-related need for, 64–66
cost savings associated with, 62
dedicated systems, 69–70
distribution programs for, 62–63

enterprise class solutions, 69
global
description of, 73–76
difficulties associated with, 74–75
solutions for, 76
help desk support, 68
hybrid systems, 69–70
methods of
dial up, 66–68
extended local area network, 68–69
modem, 67–68
multiple channels for, 69
reasons for, 61–62
stages of, 63–64
for telecommuters, 61
Rivest, Shamir, and Adelman cryptosystem, 112–113
Round robin domain name server techniques
description of, 87–88
recovery of, 87–88, 88f
Router attacks, 141

S
Scalability, of Internet
description of, 47–49
future of, 183
Security, for extranet and Internet
attack types, 19t
authentication practices and procedures
description of, 100–101
host to host, 107
individual characteristics, 101–102
passwords. See Password authentication
protocol
possession of object, 101–102
third party trust model, 106–107
types of, 101
confidentiality policies, 97–100
cryptographic solutions
description of, 108–109
encryption, 108–109
exportation of, 114
factors that affect strength of, 110
public key, 109
secret key, 109
definition of, 97
description of, 15–16, 184
ethical solutions to, 118–119
example of, 120–121

Security, for extranet and Internet *(Continued)*
   firewalls
      description of, 16–17, 51–52, 114–115
      gateways, 115–117
      host based, 117
      indications for, 20
      packet filter, 115
      performance effects of, 22–23, 46
      security attacks, 16–17, 19t, 51–52
      virus transfer across, 51–52
   global, 73–74
   information policies, 97–100
   levels of, 188
   limitations on consumer responsibility, 49–50
   logs, 17
   overview of, 119–120
   paradigms, 71–72
   perceptions regarding, 49–50
   programs, elements of, 16
   tunneling, 117–118
Serial line interface protocol, 9
SLIP. *See* Serial line interface protocol
Standards
   of computing architecture, 43–44
   international differences in, 75
Systems administrators, 37
Systems operators, 37

T
TCP/IP networking
   costs of, 13, 18
   layers, 18t–19t
   name resolution to, for load balancing of extranet, 145
   security attacks, 19t
Telecommunications services, international differences in cost of, 75–76
Telecommuting
   cost savings of, 62
   remote access for. *See* Remote access
Thin clients, vs. fat clients, 41–42, 44
Thin server, vs. fat server, 44–45

Third party trust model, of authentication, 106–107
Transaction fee, 154
Transmission Control Protocol/Internet Protocol networking. *See* TCP/IP networking
Tunneling, 117–118
   as cost driver of using Internet as an extranet, 20–21
   description of, 20–21
   effect on performance, 46
   indications for, 20
   initial cost estimate templates for, 26t–30t
   virus transfer using, 51–52
   voluntary, 46

U
Upgrading, of remote software, 143–145
Usage fee, 154
User accounts, 153
User lists, 72
Users
   access considerations, 39
   casual, 37
   end. *See* End users
   power, 37

V
Virtual private network. *See also* Extranet
   access. *See* Access
   architecture considerations, 41–43
   Internet as, 2–3
   performance considerations, 45–47
   programmer productivity, 45
   security. *See* Security
   standards of, 43–44
VPN. *See* Virtual private network

W
Web-enabled applications
   description of, 23
   development of, 23–25
   example of, 24
Web sites, implementation of, 82–83

Other Books from Digital Press

Building an Optimizing Compiler by Robert Morgan
1997   300pp   pb   1-55558-179-X

Integrating E-Mail: From the Intranet to the Internet by Simon Collin
December 1998   200pp   pb   1-55558-198-6

IPv6: The Next Generation Internet Protocol by Stewart S. Miller
1997   288pp   pb   1-55558-188-9

Oracle8 in Windows NT by Lilian Hobbs
1998   350pp   pb   1-55558-190-0

SQL Server 6.5: Performance Optimization and Tuning by Ken England
1997   250pp   pb   1-55558-180-3

TCP/IP Explained by Philip Miller
1996   450pp   pb   1-55558-166-8

Windows NT/95 for UNIX Professionals by Donald Merusi
1997   200pp   pb   1-55558-181-1

X.400 and SMTP: Battle of the E-mail Protocols by John Rhoton
1997   206pp   pb   1-55558-165-X

. . . .

Feel free to visit our web site at: http://www.bh.com/digitalpress

These books are available from all good bookstores or in case of difficulty call:
1-800-366-2665 in the U.S. or +44-1865-310366 in Europe.

E-MAIL MAILING LIST

An e-mail mailing list giving information on latest releases, special promotions, offers and other news relating to Digital Press titles is available. To subscribe, send an e-mail message to majordomo@world.std.com.
Include in message body (not in subject line): subscribe digital-press